Ordained Local Ministry

Ordained Local Ministry

A New Shape for Ministry in the Church of England

Edited by
Malcolm Torry
and
Jeffrey Heskins

CANTERBURY
PRESS
Norwich

© The Contributors 2006

First published in 2006 by the Canterbury Press Norwich
(a publishing imprint of Hymns Ancient & Modern
Limited, a registered charity)
9–17 St Albans Place, London N1 0NX

www.scm-canterburypress.co.uk

British Library Cataloguing in Publication data

A catalogue record for this book is available
from the British Library

ISBN 1-85311-723-4
978-1-85311-723-7

Typeset by Regent Typesetting, London

Printed and bound in Great Britain by
William Clowes Ltd, Beccles, Suffolk

Contents

Acknowledgements

We would like to thank those many people who have been willing to talk to us or correspond with us as we have prepared our chapters; those who have commented on our drafts; and particularly Christine Smith of the Canterbury Press for her enthusiasm for this project.

We are grateful to Church House Publishing for permission to reprint in Appendix 1 two pages from *Stranger in the Wings: A Report on Local Non-Stipendiary Ministry* (1998); and to those who have helped us with the statistics that appear in Chapter 12 and Appendix 2.

Foreword

The ordained ministry of the Church of England, while keeping its essential character, has developed during the last few decades. It is in many ways hard to imagine that up until the late 1950s the ordained ministry was only open to those with university degrees.

The formation of the Southwark Ordination Course in the 1960s opened training for ordained ministry to people in full-time employment, and in some cases to people with non-academic backgrounds.

The next stage was the recognition that in what was an increasingly secular age ordination remained closed to the average working-class Christian.

A debate started about the possibility of opening up a new model of priesthood to individuals called from within the local parish. The idea that there could be openings for people called from within the worshipping congregation to minister to their own communities by remaining local and ordained was, and still is, a radical step for the Church of England to consider.

The origins of what came to be called Ordained Local Ministry are rooted in the Stepney area of the Diocese of London and in the Diocese of Southwark. In the latter case the 'Brandon Scheme', which is described in this book, developed a model that since its inception in 1980 has grown into a programme that is open to people from all walks of life and from all types of parish.

In this book the writers describe the inception of Ordained Local Ministry (OLM) within the Diocese of Southwark. The history and development of the OLM programme are fully explored. The reflections include contributions from those who have been ordained and from the team responsible for the practice-based training course in the diocese.

The Diocese of Southwark, from which these essays come, was a pioneer in this style of ministerial training, which led to the development of other schemes in other dioceses. At the present time in the Church of England some dioceses are ending their OLM schemes, others are adopting them for the first time and in yet others, like the Diocese of Southwark, there is a continuous process

of examination to see whether the OLM pattern of ministry provides the flexibility and resilience needed for ministry in the world
of today and tomorrow.

The catholic nature of priesthood opens up the question as to
what is local. In the essays the writers explore the fact that ordination is into the worldwide Church while in Ordained Local
Ministry it is worked out in the local community in which the
priest has been nurtured and supported. Personally I remain to be
convinced by this argument but it is carefully presented.

The good practice described in these essays offers important
insights into the strengths and weaknesses of ordaining people
into their own communities, and is a helpful resource for those
planning the shape of future ministry. Whatever that pattern might
be, the experience of access for those of a non-academic background, theology rooted in the context of ministry, and the
involvement of the whole congregation in the training for ministry,
have something to teach every level of ministerial training today.

I welcome the publication of this series of essays as an important
contribution to debate on the future of ordained ministry within
the Church of England, and I hope that many people will find the
book useful.

The Rt Revd Tom Butler
Bishop of Southwark

About the Contributors

Pat Alden is an Ordained Local Minister (OLM) and now works on the Southwark Ordained Local Ministry Training Scheme as a year tutor. She is an honorary curate in the Parish of St Giles with St Matthew, Camberwell, and a consultant on religious education for the Borough of Kensington and Chelsea. Before retirement, she taught at an inner-city comprehensive school. She is a GCSE exam moderator and vice-chair of Governors at Archbishop Michael Ramsey Technical College.

Nigel Godfrey is Principal of the Southwark Ordained Local Ministry Scheme, following 20 years as an inner-city vicar in Brixton. Prior to ordination, he worked as a town planner and comes from a farming community in the Isle of Man.

Jeffrey Heskins is Rector of St Luke's and St Thomas's, Charlton. Before that, he was Curate of St Mary's, Primrose Hill, Curate of St Mary's, Enfield Chase and Enfield Deanery Youth Officer, and Team Vicar in the Kidbrooke Team Ministry. He is the author of *Unheard Voices* (Darton, Longman and Todd, 2001) and of *Face to Face* (SCM Press, 2005).

Stephen Lyon worked in Hull, Devon and Kingston upon Thames before becoming the first Principal of the Southwark Ordained Local Ministry Scheme in 1992. After eight fulfilling years in this post, he joined the staff of the Archbishops' Council with responsibility for the Church of England's links with other parts of the world Church.

Geoff Mason is a Director of Ordinands in the Diocese of Southwark. Prior to that he was Bishop's Adviser for Ministry Development, and had previously served in a variety of inner-city parishes within the Diocese of Southwark.

Arthur Obiora has belonged to St Catherine's, Hatcham (at New Cross in South London) for most of his adult life. He was ordained as an Ordained Local Minister (OLM) in 1995. He was a magistrate with the Inner London Bench and is currently a manager at the Department for Work and Pensions. He has written *Partnership in the Body of Christ* (Minerva Press, 1998).

Alyson Peberdy is Vicar of St Saviour, Brockley Hill, a single-church parish that enjoys the ministry of an Ordained Local Minister (OLM) who has lived in the area all his life. She is a member of the Southwark Diocese Ordained Local Ministry Council, and during her curacy in Oxford diocese was a tutor on the Ordained Local Ministry Scheme there. She is currently a part-time postgraduate student in theology at King's College, London.

Judith Roberts is Vice-Principal of the Southwark Ordained Local Ministry Scheme. Alongside this she works as a BACP accredited counsellor, and prior to this she was a headteacher of an inner-city primary school. She is licensed to St Michael's Church, Barnes and, by extension, to the Barnes team ministry.

Ted Roberts was Vicar of St James-the-Less, Bethnal Green, and St Mark, Victoria Park, from 1961 to 1978, and Vicar of St James and St Anne, Bermondsey, from 1982 to 1990. He then became the Bishop of Southwark's Adviser on Urban Ministry and helped to establish the Ordained Local Ministry Scheme in the diocese.

Eileen Serbutt was a secondary school English teacher, a head-teacher, and a lecturer in school management at universities in Finland, Sweden and the UK. In 2001 she was ordained as an Ordained Local Minister (OLM) for the Parish of St Mary and St John the Divine, Balham. In 2002 she became Placement Supervisor for the Southwark Diocesan Ordained Local Ministry Scheme, and in 2003 Team Facilitator Co-ordinator. She is married to a naval architect, and has one son who is a Salvation Army captain in Northern Ireland.

Grahame Shaw is Vicar of St Paul's, Newington, in Walworth. Before that he was a curate at St Andrew's, Grange, in the Diocese of Chester, then Team Vicar at East Runcorn with Halton, and then a Team Vicar in the Thamesmead team ministry.

Malcolm Torry is Team Rector in the East Greenwich Team Ministry, Vicar of St George's, Westcombe Park, chaplain to the Tate and Lyle refinery on Greenwich Peninsula, and Site Chaplain to the new development on the peninsula. Before ordination he worked for the Department of Health and Social Security. Following ordination he was curate at St Matthew's, Newington, at the Elephant and Castle, then Curate at Christ Church, Southwark, and Industrial Chaplain with the South London Industrial Mission, and then Vicar of St Catherine's, Hatcham, at New Cross. He is married and has three children. He is the editor of *The Parish* (Canterbury Press, 2004) and *Diverse Gifts* (Canterbury Press, 2006); and the author of *Managing God's Business: Religious and Faith-based Organizations and their Management* (Ashgate, 2005).

Introduction

MALCOLM TORRY AND JEFFREY HESKINS

During the late 1980s and early 1990s four new training schemes were established in the Church of England, in the Dioceses of Lincoln, Manchester, Southwark and Truro. Our experience is of the Southwark Scheme, and this book is a reflection of that experience. The contributors include Ordained Local Ministers (OLMs), incumbents of candidates, teachers of modules, a Director of Ordinands, the course Principal and Vice-Principal, a council member, and people involved in the Scheme's history.

We have written this book about the Ordained Local Ministry because, while there is a 1998 Advisory Board for Ministry report available[1] (based on a questionnaire sent to OLMs), there is nothing in a more accessible style, written by people closely involved with this particular ministry. In this book the chapters on the history are written by those closely involved in the events recounted; the chapters on selection, ministry teams, the incumbent's view, and the current training course are written by people experienced in these aspects of this ministry; and the central chapters are based on interviews with candidates and with experienced OLMs.

We anticipate that the principal readers of this book will be found in parishes and among candidates considering Ordained Local Ministry. They might also be Directors of Ordinands, Examining Chaplains and selectors; Directors of Continuing Ministerial Education; bishops, archdeacons and others in dioceses that have Ordained Local Ministry Schemes or are thinking about them – and anyone interested in the Church of England's parishes and ministry. But we also hope that others might be moved to spend some time in its pages looking at what we think has been a quiet revolution in the ordained ministry of the English Church.

The process of writing this book has been similar to that employed in writing *The Parish*[2] (an exploration of various aspects of the Church of England's parishes) and *Diverse Gifts*[3] (on the different kinds of ministry in the Church of England). Brief summaries of the chapters were prepared, and then complete drafts. These were then circulated to all of the authors, who met for a day to comment on each other's work and to discuss the content of the concluding chapter. Then the chapters were finalized and the Conclusion written. So the book can either be read as a single exploration of Ordained Local Ministry or as separate essays on aspects of that ministry.

As with the other two books, this is not an objective survey. It is based in the Diocese of Southwark and it is written on the basis of the authors' own experience and their consultations with others. We hope that by writing about our own particular situation we shall encourage our readers to reflect on their own experience, to make links, and to discover and think about differences. We also hope to see new writing on the Ordained Local Ministry from different perspectives.

We are aware as we write that our society is changing, that the Church is changing, and that the selection, training and continuing education of the ordained ministry is changing. What we offer is a snapshot of a particular place at a particular time, and in a changing world, which will mean that the reader will sometimes find occasional contradictions between theory and practice or between one practice and another. Change creates anomalies, and anomalies create further change and thus yet further anomalies.

As well as describing the history of Southwark's Scheme and offering an insight into current training and practice, we offer occasional questions about how Ordained Local Ministry might evolve. By the time our work is published, some of these questions might have been answered.

We would like to thank all those who have contributed: the authors, those who submitted to interview, and those many people who have commented on our drafts. Particular thanks are due to Christine Smith of the Canterbury Press for her enthusiastic support throughout.

A note about terminology

At various times the ministry under discussion has been called 'Local Non-Stipendiary Ministry' (LNSM), 'Local Ordained Ministry' (LOM) and 'Ordained Local Ministry' (OLM). Because it is a positive description and because the ministry is an ordained ministry experienced locally (rather than a local ordination), the current description is 'Ordained Local Ministry' (OLM), and Ordained Local Ministers are referred to as OLMs. We use this designation throughout the book even though other terms would have been used during the periods to which the historical chapters relate.

Notes

1 *Stranger in the Wings: A Report on Local Non-Stipendiary Ministry*, Advisory Board of Ministry Policy Paper no. 8, Church House Publishing, London, 1998.

2 Torry, Malcolm (ed.), *The Parish: People, Place and Ministry: A Theological and Practical Exploration*, Canterbury Press, Norwich, 2004.

3 Torry, Malcolm (ed.), *Diverse Gifts: Forms of Ministry in the Church of England*, Canterbury Press, Norwich, 2006.

1. From Here, Trained Here, Staying Here: Still an Experiment?

MALCOLM TORRY

> And after they had appointed elders for them in each church, with prayer and fasting they entrusted them to the Lord in whom they had come to believe. (Acts 14.23)

Soon after I became Vicar of St Catherine's, Hatcham, in New Cross in South London, I was talking to Ted Roberts, then living in the diocese. I had a copy of his book, *Partners and Ministers*,[1] and he was telling me about a new training scheme for Ordained Local Ministers (OLMs) in the Diocese of Southwark. Were we interested? Yes, of course we were interested: and when the selection process started, the PCC welcomed Geoff Mason, the Diocesan Ministry Development Adviser (who had been appointed to choose appropriate parishes and to help them to select candidates), to a meeting at St Catherine's, and Arthur Obiora's selection followed.

Arthur had lived in that parish and been a member of the church community since he was a student, and as he approaches retirement he's still there. He's the classic OLM. And typically that's not all that he is. He and his wife Lovedalia have two (now grown-up) children, he works as an adminstrator in the civil service, and he's a magistrate. During the first year of the Scheme everyone was feeling their way, but for the parishes and their candidates the three years of the course were a time of exploration and often of excitement. Arthur threw himself into the course: the placements, the evening meetings of candidates with tutors, and the exercises in the parish. One particularly tricky moment was when he became so committed to his placement in our local youth club that we had to work hard to extract him from it. Arthur was ordained deacon in 1995 and priest in 1996. Taking it in turns with Francis Makambwe, the parish's current incumbent, he presides at the Eucharist and preaches, and involves himself pastorally in the community and congregation.

And now I'm experiencing it all over again. I'm now Vicar of St George's, Westcombe Park, in the Parish of East Greenwich. Cynthia Finnerty had been here for 30 years, living round the corner from the parish church. Her husband Eddie is churchwarden, and she is the parish musician. She seems to know everyone and everything. She was the natural and immediate choice when the Church Council sought a candidate for ordination: her leadership gifts are unmistakable, and her commitment to the community and the congregation are profound. She will make a fine priest in this community.

This book is about a Church of England ministry: a ministry that is both ordained and local. It is also a non-stipendiary ministry, which is why it was first called LNSM – Local Non-Stipendiary Ministry – rather than OLM, Ordained Local Ministry.

In one sense, of course, the history of this ministry goes back nearly 2,000 years. Paul was an itinerant church-planter and the apostles who ended up in Jerusalem had been deployed from Galilee, but as far as we can tell the leaderships of the churches Paul planted and the 'elders', 'overseers' and 'deacons' mentioned in the New Testament's later letters were local people whose leadership gifts had been recognized by their congregations and by the apostles. But by the twentieth century, the normal ordained ministry in the Church of England was middle-class, university-educated, and deployable from place to place.

It was the early history, and a recognition that there were leadership gifts and possibly vocations to the ordained ministry among people who didn't fit the current model of ordained leadership in the Church of England, that led to the early modern experiments in recognizing vocations locally, training people locally and, on ordination, licensing them to serve in the communities where they belonged.

It is the 'locality' that was new (or rather, which was a return to an earlier model). While the Bernard Gilpin Society and Brasted College (residential colleges in Durham and Kent) and subsequently the Aston Scheme (a part-time scheme based in Birmingham) had been preparing men without university education for the rigours of theological college, and Kelham Theological College had trained a number of working-class candidates, the men trained there became stipendiary clergy and normally didn't return to their original communities.

What might have been an experiment in Local Ordained Ministry, but in the end wasn't, was the Southwark Ordination Course, established in 1962. This course trained men from a variety of employments and backgrounds on a part-time basis, and many of those men remained both in their employments upon ordination and in the parishes from which they came. What mattered to Bishops Mervyn Stockwood and John Robinson, to the course, and to the men concerned, was that this was a way of opening the ordained ministry to a group of men either unable or unwilling to undertake full-time training. The training course was from the beginning to be as academic in its educational method as any full-time theological college, and it quickly became a means of training people from mainly middle-class backgrounds for both stipendiary and non-stipendiary ministry. This course (currently the South-East Institute for Theological Education) and similar courses now produce clergy who expect *not* to return to their original parishes.

The experiments in Stepney in the Diocese of London (see Chapter 2), and in the Brandon area of Walworth in the Diocese of Southwark (Chapter 3), were genuine attempts to break the mould. Here men were selected locally, with their parishes involved in the selection; they were trained locally; and they were ordained to serve in the parishes from which they came. From these experiments lessons were learnt, and when four new courses started in the Dioceses of Lincoln and Manchester in the late 1980s, and in Southwark and Truro in the early 1990s, and the General Synod's Advisory Board for Ministry issued its first policy paper in an attempt to regulate them, it was clear that the new approach was no longer just an experiment. In all four cases both parish and candidate were selected together, and criteria for selection were that the parish be seen to be practising some form of collaborative ministry and that the candidate would be supported by their church community which would also participate in the training process. Furthermore, in a significant departure from other selection criteria, the candidate was to have been part of their community and congregation for an appreciable length of time, and was to be committed to staying within it. This was all new.

As the book *The Parish*[2] shows, a parish is its community, its territory, its congregation, its parish church and its ministry. So when we say that a candidate for the Ordained Local Ministry must have been in their parish for some length of time and must intend to stay there, 'parish' here means both the congregation and the community at large. Similarly, when we say that the parish is involved in the candidate's selection, we mean that a profile of the community and the territory is part of the process and that another part of it is the congregation being involved in the selection through the PCC. And when we say that the parish participates in the candidate's training, we mean both that the congregation participates in it in various ways and that some of it is done in the context of the wider community – as we shall see.

Trained here

Much of the training is in the candidate's parish – a neighbourhood profile, work on pastoral care, a mission statement, preaching, leading worship – all designed to prepare the candidate for the task of being a priest in that particular place. (It is no contradiction that the candidate disappears from their own parish for several weeks during the second year of training to spend time in another parish very different from their own: for this exercise gives a new perspective which enables them to be more objective about their own parish and thus to serve it better.)

A major innovation is the educational method, which is more practice-based than theory-based. It is *fairly* true to say that most training for the ordained ministry follows the academic model: that is, theory is studied and is then applied in practice. Thus we find courses made up mainly of lectures, seminars, reading and the writing of essays, with placements and practical exercises fitted into the gaps. With the Ordained Local Ministry course in the Diocese of Southwark, it is rather different. Yes, candidates do come together once a week, and there are modules on the New Testament, Christian doctrine, liturgy, etc., but these sessions are designed around practice. I can only write knowledgeably about the Christian Doctrine module which I teach, but here, in a subject that is normally thought of as academic and theory-laden, it is all practical exercises: scouring the Scriptures for connections and meanings, developing techniques to grasp the meaning of ancient doctrinal texts, using role-plays to explore the use and development of doctrinal ideas in evangelistic and pastoral settings, and holding formal debates to hone apologetic skills.

Placements in secular institutions, parishes and chaplaincies are at the heart of the course and take up large chunks of core time in all three years; and study weekends and study days are spent on the skills and knowledge that a priest needs.

I have written at length about the training course because it is the establishment of the training courses by the dioceses (and there are now 18 such courses) that has been the driving force in the development of Ordained Local Ministry. In order to establish this style of ministry, dioceses had to establish training schemes and these had to be regularized and regulated. But now, 15 years on, the focus is changing. There are now hundreds of OLMs (nearly

100 in the Diocese of Southwark alone), and their ministry is experienced in a considerable proportion of the parishes of the diocese.

Staying here

These clergy are local: they come from their parishes, and they serve where they came from, thus complementing the ministry of the incumbent who will normally not come from there and won't be staying there – at least, not for long.

It is this ministry that this book is all about. There are chapters on the early experiments in Stepney and Walworth, and on the establishment of the training scheme in the Diocese of Southwark (from the Principal at the time, and from a participant). The two central chapters, by Jeffrey Heskins, are in many ways the heart of the book because they offer the current experience of OLMs. One of these chapters is based on interviews with OLMs, and the other on interviews with candidates currently in their third year of training. Chapters follow on a variety of perspectives on Ordained Local Ministry: on the incumbent's eye view, on ministry teams, on selection, on the training course, and on a particular aspect of the course important to parishes, candidates and course staff: the achievement of potential.

My own desire to gather a group of contributors stems from my experience of Ordained Local Ministry. At my last parish in New Cross and in my current parish of East Greenwich, we have had candidates for Ordained Local Ministry. I have been an Examining Chaplain and an Area Director of Ordinands, and in these roles have helped to select candidates and their parishes. I have been a personal tutor to candidates, I have been on the training scheme's council, and I teach a module on the course.

Why? Because I believe that Ordained Local Ministry is here to stay, that it has something important to offer to the Church of England's parishes and to their communities and congregations (and not least its connection with early Christian practice). And maybe in time this type of ministry will become a normative ordained ministry, if not *the* normative one.

Yes, of course there are questions to be asked. Are the candidates sufficiently trained? What do we mean by 'local' now that many of us spend different parts of our lives in different places and in different networks? Because they have been in one place for a long time and will be staying in that place, might OLMs become rather blinkered? And now that so many of our communities are changing so fast and are increasingly multi-ethnic and multicultural, is someone who has been in a parish a long time and intends to stay there necessarily the best person to be a priest in that community?

After reading the chapters of this book, the reader might like to decide whether their authors have answered these questions.

It won't be very long before we can evaluate the experience of a whole generation of OLMs and compare that evaluation with other forms of ordained ministry – and in a cash-strapped Church an important part of that evaluation must be the relative costs of training and of sustaining an Ordained Local Ministry.

In the meantime, we offer this book as our own appreciation of the many who in the past and more recently have caught a vision and made sure it happened. Yes, this book is about a particular place, and it makes no claims to objectivity or universality, but that is as it should be, for Ordained Local Ministry is by its nature different in every place. Our readers will be able to make connections between what we have written and their own situation, and they will be able to spot the differences and ask about their meanings and consequences. We hope that what we have written will encourage others to write out of their own experience, and that what they write will be very different from what we have written. For just as we expect the Church in each country to be formed by the Christian faith in its historical diversity and unity *and* by the culture of that country, so we should expect the Church in each community to be shaped by the faith and practice of the Church universally and by the culture of that particular community. No one can know that culture better than someone who has been there for 30 years, so such a person could have much to offer as a representative and pastoral figure in the community and in the worshipping congregation. The Christian faith is incarnational: its heart is God come in the flesh in a particular place and at a particular time, and its life today is discipleship in the particular places in which we find ourselves. The Ordained Local Ministry will, in the end, be judged on its contribution to the worship and mission of the Church in its parishes.

The Ordained Local Ministry is both old and young. It is the original pattern of the Church's ministry; and it has been part of the pattern of ministry in the Church of England for the past 15 years. Whether we should still regard it as an experiment, we shall have to leave our readers to decide once they've read the rest of the book.

Further reading

Advisory Board of Ministry, *Strangers in the Wings: A Report on Local Non-Stipendiary Ministry*, Church House Publishing, London, 1998.

Russell, Anthony, *The Clerical Profession*, SPCK, London, 1980.

Notes

1 Roberts, Ted, *Partners and Ministers: An Experiment in Supplementary Ministry*, Falcon Books, London, 1972.

2 Torry, Malcolm (ed.), *The Parish: People, Place and Ministry: A Theological and Practical Exploration*, Canterbury Press, London, 2004.

2. A Novelty, or Back to Basics? The Bethnal Green and Bermondsey Experiments

TED ROBERTS

There is no longer Jew or Greek, there is no longer slave or free, there is no longer male and female; for all of you are one in Christ Jesus. (Galatians 3.28)

'Can a docker be a clergyman in the Church of England?' I used those words in 1969 to explain a scheme we devised in East London. Indeed, the scheme's aim was to ask just that question.

In 1968 Trevor Huddleston had come from Masasi in Tanzania to be our bishop. I soon discovered that we shared a passion –the hope of creating an indigenous Church. I was convinced that, in the great urban areas of Britain, for the Church to take root it must grow out of, and belong in, the local community. Trevor had come to the same conclusion in rural Africa. Overseas it had long been accepted that if a genuinely indigenous Church is to grow, then it must have an indigenous ministry, but in Britain we were slow to accept that principle. We had failed to see that working-class people are best equipped to lead the Church in the working-class areas of our cities.

St Mark, Victoria Park, is in Bow, St James-the-Less in Bethnal Green. Only two stations on the Underground east of the City of London, but in another world. Its people were the proud inheritors of the true Cockney tradition. The old terraced houses had been replaced by modern flats, the children were well dressed, and people are enjoying some long overdue affluence. This much was obvious even to a casual observer, but it took a little longer to discover that East Londoners believed that their way of life had its own distinctive character and that it was as enjoyable and valid as any other. For the majority, the Church did not constitute part of that life.

The records of many East London parishes bore witness to great achievements by earlier generations. Even in the darkest days of the Depression, God was glorified by triumphs achieved in his name. But these achievements had been almost exclusively with individuals. For some reason we had failed to create Christian community. The Church simply had not taken root in East London. It seemed to some of us then that if a way could be found to put responsibility for leadership into the hands of people who belonged in East London, then maybe we could make progress towards establishing a Church that belonged.

We asked for men (at that time it could only be men) to begin training. One was a retired docker, one a telephone engineer, one a roofer, and one a service engineer for business machines. They understood that their call had to be confirmed, first by the local church and then by the existing Anglican procedures. The following year every member of both congregations was asked to express an opinion about the fitness of these four men to serve as their ministers. Questions about the scheme were collected and answered and the men themselves were questioned publicly during a Sunday service. We all felt very vulnerable, but we began to understand one part of the New Testament as we had never done before. When Jesus began his public ministry, those among whom he had grown up said: 'Surely this is Jesus, Joseph's son! We know his father and mother' (John 6.42). Vulnerability is painful, but it was a small price to pay for the knowledge of being accepted by those who know you best. The local church approved each of the four, and they attended an Advisory Council for the Church's Ministry (ACCM) Selection Conference which recommended them for training. They were made deacon in 1972 and ordained priest in 1974.

That is the simple outline of a scheme that would not now appear to be as revolutionary as we felt it to be then.

What were we hoping to achieve? Was what we then proposed new? Were we really being revolutionary, or simply trying to return to New Testament principles?

What were we hoping to achieve?

I believe that the ministry we tried to encourage in East London grew out of New Testament principles, but why was it necessary to depart from established patterns?

What is an Anglican clergyman?

Most would answer that he or she will have been trained in a college, will be a professional, and that ministry will be that person's full-time paid work. The minister will stay in one parish for five or ten years and then move on, and will expect eventually to be in sole charge of a parish.

This pattern of ministry has served the Church well, but we have no right to suppose that this professional ministry should be our only form. The Bible speaks of 'varieties of ministries'. There were itinerant ministers in the New Testament, some of whom were paid by the local church and some of whom earned their own living; but a local church would never have regarded those who came in temporarily from somewhere else as 'the ministry', as we have come to do. It was expected that each church would produce its own ministers from within its own membership. In arguing for a team of part-time ministers we were not arguing against the full-time clergyman. The New Testament pattern is one of variety, fluidity, openness to change. We should not impose upon ourselves an invariable pattern of hierarchy when there is an exciting and liberating alternative.

Was what we proposed new?

At the time it was different from the existing model in six ways:

1 A team rather than solitary ministers

A team would share the ministry. Different people would bring different gifts. We hoped those gifts would complement one another rather than relying on one person to be omnipotent.

2 Called by the local church

The congregation was encouraged to see these clergy as belonging. They had called them both to the ministry and to their parish.

3 Settled rather than itinerant

Traditionally, clergy move from place to place during their ministry. These men were born and bred in the streets where they were to minister and would expect to stay there.

4 Training local and practical

We planned that they would train locally rather than asking them
to go away to college. They could keep their jobs and continue to
help in bringing up their families.

In addition, we wanted to attract men to the ministry who might
be ill at ease with exams and the professional style of training, but
would be at home with apprenticeship, since that is how they had
trained for their jobs.

5 A specific term of service

It is generally accepted that ordination commits a person to the
work of ministry for life. We planned that our local ordinands
would accept a limit of seven years on their licence, when they
would be at liberty to resign and might or might not take up their
ministry again, then or later.

Working-class men are not used to the idea of jobs that have a
lifelong commitment, and could find the idea suffocating. A seven-
year licence would not affect the fact that they were ordained for
life.

6 Voluntary rather than paid

This idea was not new, even 30 years ago, but it was important to
us to identify the boundary between vocation and profession.
Those who have a vocation do not have to become professional in
order to serve God.

The alienation of the working class

It was clear to us that for a very large proportion of the population
of England the organized Church was particularly irrelevant
because of the issue of class. To speak of class nearly always
generates heat. Many of us would like to remove the words from
our vocabulary, but before we can do that we must remove the
experience from our lives.

Paul singled out the three great divisions in society: race, class
and gender, when he said, 'There is no longer Jew or Greek, . . .
slave or free, . . . male and female; for all of you are one in Christ
Jesus' (Galatians 3.28). Some Christians would suggest that this
means that Christ has done away with the great divisions in
society, but we know from experience that that is not true. This
Scripture is saying that these divisions are all too real, they have

always been part of the fabric of society, but that a Christian should not allow them to affect their relationships with those who are of different race or gender. The Church in the great urban areas of our cities was weak because we had managed to ignore differences of class and this had encouraged the Church to reflect patterns of life that were foreign to the everyday life of people in those areas.

Bishop Ted Wickham had an interesting insight on this problem: 'The working class, whatever its transmutations, has remained the largest single social group most estranged from the churches of Europe.'[1] The one notable exception was the Roman Catholic Church. The Roman Catholic Church in Ireland was not identified with the English ruling classes, so when large groups of Irish immigrants found themselves concentrated in the worst housing areas of London, Glasgow and Liverpool, their priests were not identified with the employers. First they came from Ireland, then later from within their own urban communities. Their priesthood was indigenous.

At the beginning of the twentieth century, Charles Booth found that churches, missions and settlements could gather a respectable congregation of the poor by liberal granting of relief. The missions and settlements with their large staffs from outside the area only helped to mask the real problem: the absence of responsible adult church life. Booth writes: 'Wherever the regular working class is found . . . it seems equally impervious to the claims of religion . . . while those who do join any church become almost indistinguishable from the class with which they then mix. The change that has really come about is not so much *of* as *out of* the class to which they have belonged.'[2]

There were exceptions to this pattern of working-class alienation. Durham miners and the chapels of the Welsh valleys or Lancashire mill towns are often quoted, but these examples relate to small industrial towns. A city of half a million does not always break up into one-class areas, but a vast metropolis like London does. That was the problem we faced in East London 30 years ago. Willmott and Young[3] described East London as a vast one-class quarter. It was wrong to impose on these areas patterns of church life that reflected values more middle class than biblical and expect them to take root. We applied at home the lessons learned overseas: a strong Church will become established and will expand according to the laws of spiritual life when it is allowed to reflect those aspects of its community's own culture that are consistent with biblical principles.

The complex and emotive theme of class has probably never been described better than by Richard Hoggart in *The Uses of*

Literacy.[4] He argued that the 'educators', among whom the clergy are a significant group, will always be tempted to see a distinctive working-class culture as 'inferior', particularly if they have themselves been educated 'out of it'. Hoggart wrote in the *Observer*: 'Grammar schools can exert a great – if well meant or even unconscious – pressure to remove their working-class pupils from attachment to their homes and neighbourhoods; they tend to seek to attach them to middle-class values . . . a substantial proportion [of the teachers] not only reject their own working-class background, but reject it with scorn and adhere grimly to their new middle-class attitudes.'[5]

A similar process had been at work in the Church. Many of the clergy were themselves educated in the atmosphere described by Richard Hoggart. But whatever may or may not happen in schools, the Church is committed to the view that 'there is no longer Jew or Greek, there is no longer slave or free'. One culture is not better than the other. Both working class and middle class had their strengths and weaknesses, neither was wholly good or wholly bad. They were different.

When the Church allows itself to be geared to a certain privileged form of society, it is guilty of rejecting people. This rejection is felt, for example, if we say that a person must achieve a certain academic standard before being ordained.

Thirty years ago in East London we attempted to create a pattern of ministry that we hoped would take a step towards building a Church that would belong in the great urban areas of our cities. We believed that we were following New Testament principles and so, to that extent, we can claim that the scheme was not a novelty but an attempt to get back to basics.

Some of the principles that were important to us 30 years ago have become part of the experience of many who have been ordained since, but there was no continuing scheme in Stepney as we had hoped. In the late 1980s I was invited by the Bishop of Southwark to repeat what we had done in Bethnal Green in Bermondsey. With the support of the Diocesan Director of Ordinands, John Cox, and a neighbouring incumbent, Peter Maurice, two men, Snowy Davol and Tom Cockerton, were ordained.

Nearly half of the dioceses of the Church of England now have schemes for the training of OLMs. This is a major achievement. My one concern is that the alienation of the working class from the Church does not seem to have been given the priority it deserves.

Further reading

Roberts, Ted, *Partners and Ministers: An Experiment in Supplementary Ministry*, Falcon Books, London, 1972.

Notes

1 Wickham, E.R., in a private document.

2 Booth, Charles, *The Life and Labour of the People of London 1890–1900*, Macmillan, London, 1902.

3 Willmott, Peter, and Young, Michael, *Family and Kinship in East London*, Pelican, Harmondsworth, 1957, p. 93.

4 Hoggart, Richard, *The Uses of Literacy*, Pelican, Harmondsworth, 1957.

5 *Observer*, 11 February 1962.

3. People and Places: The Brandon Experiment

GRAHAME SHAW

Now in the church at Antioch there were prophets and teachers: Barnabas, Simeon who was called Niger, Lucius of Cyrene, Manaen a member of the court of Herod the ruler, and Saul. While they were worshipping the Lord and fasting, the Holy Spirit said, 'Set apart for me Barnabas and Saul for the work to which I have called them.' Then after fasting and praying they laid their hands on them and sent them off. (Acts 13.1–3)

The territory

In 1980, the deaneries of Southwark Diocese (which at that time did not include Croydon) were required to respond to the pastoral strategy document called *People and Places*. In the Southwark and Newington deanery (which includes Southwark, Walworth and parts of Camberwell and Kennington), we divided the territory into three parts. Our four-parish territory was called the Brandon Area because it was almost coterminous with the Brandon Estate: a Greater London Council housing area that included parts of Walworth, Camberwell and Kennington.

All four churches were post-1960s new buildings in relatively stable communities of almost 100 per cent social housing. Postwar urban renewal over 30 years had helped to secure significant population stability. This was true of the four congregations then, and this remained so until the mid-1990s.

Three of the Anglican parishes had new incumbents in their mid-thirties: Henry Morgan and myself had radical urban roots, and Dominic Walker had been the personal chaplain to the Bishop of Southwark, Mervyn Stockwood. John Whitelam was a long-serving Vicar of St Agnes, Kennington, and had overseen the rebuilding of his church, church hall and vicarage. Although there were differences of expression and practice, there had been sustained work on shared mission through a local newspaper, *Compass*, for more than a decade, a shared interest in issues facing local authority housing estates, and involvement together with church and community schools, tenants' organizations, youth centres and the scouting movement.

There was a history of liaison between the four full-time clergy but, although two parishes, St Michael's and St Paul's, were an established group ministry, there was animated opposition to the concept of a formal team ministry. 'Too much yakking', a parishioner commented.

Also in 1980, at a Deanery Synod meeting, we noted that there was only one Southwark Pastoral Auxiliary and one potential Reader in the deanery. At a different meeting, an incandescent lay training officer told us off about this. I think he was right to do it, but wrong in his analysis. What was needed was local *ordained* leadership.

Beginning

People and Places: A Pastoral Strategy for Mission,[1] produced by the Joint Advisory Group of the Southwark Diocese, sought local responses to sections on 'the need for new patterns of ministry' and on a recommendation that 'training ministries' be set up in each deanery.

In the initial meeting of the four clergy to discuss *People and Places*, we discussed the situations we found ourselves in (two incumbents had arrived within the year) and where we understood our parishes to be in their development and medium-term future. Our conversation moved to sharing knowledge of people who had expressed interest in ordained ministry. One of our number, while being appropriately discreet, knew the realities of diocesan selection processes, but we were all aware that the men we were suggesting were likely to be rejected by a national selection conference.

South-east London had seen a variety of training for ordained ministry, and we ourselves had experience of various kinds of training. I had been a student at the Bernard Gilpin Society (a pre-theological college college) and two other deanery incumbents had been in similar training. Before I came to Walworth I had been on the staff of the Parish of Thamesmead where I had been involved with two student placements from Westcott and Cuddesdon Theological Colleges. Three of us were involved with tutorial support of students. At St Matthew's at the Elephant and Castle there had for many years been an urban placement for nearly all students at the Salisbury and Wells Theological College. The Southwark Ordination Course was based at Christ Church, Blackfriars, which was in the deanery, and some of us had been involved in teaching on the course and in tutoring students. On the basis of this experience we were aware that the men we had in mind might not fit into established training patterns.

But good news travels fast, and we were aware of the imaginative work that Ted Roberts had undertaken in Bethnal Green, and this seemed to be a useful model to follow.

We resolved to record our conversation and to request that a new approach to Local Ordained Ministry should be tried in the Brandon Area. This would be distinct from the Southwark Ordination Course and would be based in our parishes. We discussed the plan with our respective PCCs and in 1980 the 'gang of twenty' emerged – four laypeople and one priest from each parish, to act as a steering group. (This was the era of the 'gang of four' who had left the Labour Party to form the Social Democratic Party.) The gang of twenty led to a good deal of solidarity and local commitment to the scheme during its gestation.

Preparing

The emerging candidates were Ben Moakes, Peter Smith, Ted Dawson, John Wash and Sonny Brown. Five candidates from one close-knit urban deanery was a unique experience, and Chapter 11 sheds light on some of the issues facing those who managed the selection process. Questions were asked: Is it possible for people locally called and permanently licensed to one parish to move to another parish? Would ordaining local volunteers mean that full-time posts would be withdrawn? Would it lead to more clericalism? But all were selected, and the early stages of their training was marked by a 'commissioning' by Bishop Mervyn just before he retired. He recalled that, when the Southwark Ordination Course had been established during the early years of his episcopate, he had hoped that it would train more 'local' clergy. Now he was seeing that happen.

At the beginning of the Brandon training, the Canon Missioner Richard Garrard was assigned to the overall task of training and supervision of the five candidates. He had been involved with Church Army Officer training, and he put this experience to good use, constructing a course with plenty of practical experience in it, along with reflection on that experience. Most of the training was in the immediate locality and was adapted to the capacity of the candidates and of their incumbents. Key terms used in a description of the training were 'apprenticeship', 'cohesion' and 'mutual support'. Other resources were employed as necessary. For instance, the candidates attended part of a Reader training module: same training, different destination.

Outcome

The candidates were ordained deacon in 1981 (during their training) and priest in 1983 (though John Wash's ordination as a priest was slightly delayed: a pragmatic decision relating to a family member's illness). By the time he was ordained, Ben Moakes, the most experienced candidate in terms of offices held, was over 75 years old. Did the passage of time or the gracious turning of a blind eye ordain him? His ordination happened and he was an active priest for ten years. He died in harness, holding in a long life many of the responsibilities of urban parish life, ending as an OLM.

At the same time as the area was coming to terms with a new style of ordained ministry, a major context change emerged as a new area bishop arrived and incumbents changed. There was a determined attempt to establish a team ministry with three stipendiary clergy and four of the ordained local clergy. This led to the end of the group ministry that had generated significant ecumenical relationships and also a commitment to the ordination of women as priests. St Paul's was unable to go along with the team ministry proposal. The Brandon Scheme was affected. All of the ordained local clergy wished to work collectively, but now there were tensions between their parishes, not least because of the growing debate over whether women could be ordained priest. Ted Dawson, at St Paul's, took a sabbatical, and eventually moved to St John's, Walworth, the parish in which he lived. He subsequently developed a hospital chaplaincy ministry. But whatever the tensions, the group of five continued to support each other, particularly when their parishes were between full-time incumbents.

John Wash remained an OLM at St Mary's, Newington, until 2004 when he retired to Cyprus; Peter Smith moved from St Michael's, Camberwell, in 1995 and was licensed as an OLM at St John's, Croydon; and Sonny Brown, who is now a Chelsea Pensioner and in his nineties, still presides regularly at St Agnes, Kennington. He is the last practising Brandon Scheme OLM.

It is frequently turbulent in urban areas, and not only because of the turbulence that the whole of the Church of England has faced during the period in question. Staff changes in particular can con-tribute to the difficulties that parishes face. One of the very good unplanned outcomes of the Brandon Scheme was the stability that the local ordained men brought to a number of parishes. But the major outcome has got to be that nearly 100 person-years of ordained ministry has been offered.

To this day, in what was called the Brandon Area, there remain four sustainable parishes and four full-time clergy. Each parish has promoted and supported other candidates for ministry. Within three of the parishes there have been three stipendiary women working for a joint tally of 24 years, with a minister in full-time secular employment for seven years. Further, within the Deanery of Southwark and Newington there are now four OLMs from within the present course and three stipendiary priests trained at the South-East Institute for Theological Education, the Southwark Ordination Course's successor. In the Brandon Area itself there are currently no OLMs, but new ones might emerge under God's providence.

Conclusion

In 1983 Mark Hodge wrote a report on the scheme for the Bishop of Southwark, Ronald Bowlby.[2] It had concluded that what had taken place had been radical, productive, challenging, and an indication of how Ordained Local Ministry might operate in the diocese in the future. The *Faith in the City*[3] report published in 1985 held up the Brandon Scheme and the Bethnal Green experiment as indicators of an important way forward for the ordained ministry.[4]

The Brandon Scheme was a major success, and out of it Southwark's own formal authorized scheme evolved. Great trees from little acorns grow.

Notes

1 *People and Places: A Pastoral Strategy for Mission*, Diocese of Southwark, London, 1980.

2 Hodge, Mark, *The Brandon Scheme: A Report to the Bishop of Southwark*, Ministry Development Group, Diocese of Southwark, London, 1983.

3 *Faith in the City: The Report of the Archbishop's Commission on Urban Priority Areas*, Church House Publishing, London, 1985, pp. 112f and 125f.

4 *Faith in the City*, p. 113.

4. The Changing Environment: 1970–2005

PAT ALDEN, NIGEL GODFREY
AND GEOFF MASON

You are the light of the world. A city built on a hill cannot be hidden. (Matthew 5.14)

1 The changing world: 1970–2005

A case study: St Giles with St Matthew's, Camberwell

This chapter is a look at the changing environment, both in terms of the Church and of the world, making particular reference to the Church in inner-city south London, and focusing on what is now the United Benefice of St Giles with St Matthew's, Camberwell. This parish had its first OLM priest ordained in 2003 (Pat Alden, who had been born and raised in the parish), and its second a year later, in 2004 (Isoline Russell, who had belonged to one of the first waves of migration from the West Indies into the parish).

The political landscape

The 1970s saw a shift to the political right in the Western world, and in Britain Margaret Thatcher's Conservative government was elected in 1979. On 28 March 1982 the *Observer* recorded Margaret Thatcher as saying: 'The time for counter-attack is long overdue . . . We are reaping what was sown in the sixties. The fashionable theories and permissive claptrap sets the scene for a society in which the old virtues of discipline and self-restraint were deni-grated.' Through the Thatcherite years, inner-city areas like Camberwell experienced firsthand some of this counter-attack. It was, however, nothing in comparison to the structural changes affecting areas on the Celtic fringe of the UK that were dominated by such heavy industry as the nationalized coal mining and steel industries. Adrian Hastings, writing of the 'privatization' of nationalized industries during this period, says: 'Not since the Dissolution of the Monasteries had there happened in this country so vast and reckless a public sale of property to the benefit of the very rich.'[1]

Unemployment was rife throughout the 1980s, reaching levels in excess of 25 per cent in some areas. Unemployment was particularly high among the young in inner-city areas, and among people from ethnic minorities. Camberwell, in common with many inner-city areas with high concentrations of people from ethnic minorities, suffered particularly heavy unemployment during this period. St Matthew's bordered Brixton's Coldharbour Lane area, where riots were experienced in 1981, the touchpaper being lit by a police over-reaction to a minor incident in Wiltshire Road, just beyond the parish boundary. The Commission of Inquiry that followed the riots, chaired by Lord Scarman, identified the cause of the riots as the cumulative effect of decades of discrimination against people from ethnic minorities. They experienced poorer opportunities in the housing and employment markets, and they suffered racial harassment and less than neutral policing. Positive action flowing from the Scarman Report was a long time coming, which was not surprising in the prevailing political climate.

The *Faith in the City* report was published in 1985. It made 38 recommendations to the Church of England and 23 to the government and nation. The report aimed to bring both the Church and the community in Urban Priority Areas (UPAs) back into the life of the Church and the nation. The document, critical of government policy in Urban Priority Areas such as Camberwell, was branded as Marxist, and politicians told the Church to confine itself to religion and to leave politics to others. The effect of the attack was perhaps to give greater publicity to the report, which began to make a significant difference in some inner-city areas. It led to the Church Urban Fund, which in time would distribute funds to a host of inner-city initiatives of a socio-religious nature. The fund was important for the financial support it gave, but also symbolically, for it gave hope to forgotten parts of both Church and society. It encouraged them to feel that they didn't have to accept the way the world was and could be more in control of their lives. In that sense it actually mirrored Conservative policy, which emphasized that the world did not owe you a living.

As is often the case, it was the inner-city parishes with more able laity and clergy that were able to seize some of these opportunities. St Giles was just such a parish. It established the Camberwell Choir school (a very different animal to that suggested by the name), which provided opportunities for the young to explore music and the performing arts. This was initially housed at St Matthew's, and from small beginnings it developed and is now housed at St Giles where nearly 100 children engage weekly in drama, singing, art and music lessons. The project has become a long-term feature in St Giles' parish life. Subsequently, a jazz club was also developed in the church crypt, and this still thrives. (Since the 1960s, the crypt had housed a homeless persons' project, the St Giles Trust. By the 1990s, the Trust had become well established and had moved to more appropriate premises elsewhere in Camberwell.)

Communications

Communications changed rapidly during the period 1970–2005. Car ownership continued to soar, with the M25 at capacity in places almost as soon as it was complete. The privatization of the railways at the end of the Conservative era also coincided with the time when the number of people using public transport was beginning to rise in London as changing attitudes to commuter traffic and transport policy enabled buses to have some level of priority on the roads. The A202 crosses the parish of Camberwell. Bus lanes restricted cars to a single lane; and this, along with the congestion charge in central London, introduced in February 2003, has greatly affected traffic flows in the area.

In 1970 the Surrey Docks closed when Tilbury, further downstream, became London's container port. Many basins and canals south of the river were filled in and developed by the London Docklands Development Corporation (LDDC), which was established in 1980. The Surrey canal, running to the north and east of the parish, became green walkways and parkways in and around Burgess Park in Peckham. This created much-needed green space where previously there had been industrial wasteland.

The built/natural environment

In the northern hemisphere, industrializing cities developed a west/east split, with industry and poorer communities on the east side and the more prosperous residential areas on the west side. The phenomenon was largely the result of a prevailing westerly wind blowing pollutants eastwards. Cities like London also developed in concentric rings, warped by communication systems such as railways, which brought areas further away into commuting distance of the city; while geographical factors, such as the

Thames, might act as barriers as well as communication links. The city centre business district was surrounded by an inner ring. This was initially where wealthier sections of society settled; but as the housing aged, and as new housing was built farther out, new migrant communities settled in what became the 'inner city'. These areas were in turn surrounded by inner and outer suburbs, with commuter towns beyond the green belt. People tended to move outwards as they became more prosperous. Charles Booth in the nineteenth century described south London's inner city from Deptford to Battersea as the world's 'longest stretch of unbroken poverty'. In reality, of course, the picture was more complex, as a secluded conservation area in Camberwell or neighbouring Dulwich might remain as exclusive developments housing the rich. The exclusivity might be highlighted by the fact that during the Brixton riots local people in Dulwich hamlet barricaded routes into the village, not trusting the police to be able to protect them. In the early 1970s the parish of St Giles was heavily dependent on the articulate white middle-class people who inhabited the conservation area.

In the 1970s the development pattern began to change. The high-rise estates of the 1960s that had replaced the slums of earlier years were themselves beginning to decay rapidly. The 'Right to Buy' option had never really been taken up in the vast high-rise housing estates of the inner city. To the east of St Giles parish, the huge North Peckham estate, with its aerial walkways (a rather poor interpretation of the Le Corbusier dream), was becoming a 'hard to let' dumping ground for the socially excluded. It was in this environment that Damilola Taylor was murdered in November 2000. Subsequently, Debbie Welch, the St Giles parish's ministry team chairperson, who was on the payroll of the diocese, spent a good deal of time on this estate dealing with the fall-out of this unsolved crime. She never really got over this tragedy, and she herself tragically died young. Subsequent to this appalling incident there were renewed efforts in dealing with the unsatisfactory housing conditions on such estates, so these 1960s estates in turn began to be replaced by low-rise/high-density mixed social and private housing.

High-rise residential development may still be a significant part of the built environment, especially along the banks of the River Thames, both through new build and the conversion of warehouses, but now the target group is very different: young professionals entering the private housing market prior to commencing a family, or even purchasing for investment. St Giles parish has largely been unaffected by this new kind of development, though its sought-after Victorian terrace housing is having something of a renaissance, being bought by young professionals requiring easy access to the city.

Socio-economic patterns

London's economic base since the 1970s has changed rapidly. The closure of Surrey Docks in 1970, together with its associated industries, initially meant a great deal of unemployment. Norman Tebbitt, Secretary of State for Employment's famous remark, 'My father didn't riot, he got on his bike and looked for work', summed up how inner-city people felt they were regarded by government: their needs were not understood and they were far from the centre of the political agenda. The 1980s began to see the economy turn round, and by the 1990s it was a very different kind of world. New industries arose, while manufacturing became even less significant in the economy. The service sector developed rapidly. In the City of London and further to the east in Canary Wharf, the financial sector blossomed. This was especially true after the 'big bang' of October 1986 and the computerization of the Stock Exchange. London became one of the three key financial centres alongside New York and Tokyo. It was becoming a truly global city. Besides central London and the finance sector, the service sector saw the rise of whole new industries, such as computing and software. There was also expansion of some of the older service industries such as medical services. The Parish of St Giles with St Matthew's, Camberwell, saw the expansion of King's College Hospital and the Maudsley Hospital during this period. The Maudsley evolved in association with 'care in the community' programmes: an idea that saw the demolition of so many other large Victorian psychiatric institutions throughout the UK.

Multi-faith/multicultural Britain

London has seen wave after wave of migration over the centuries. There were those associated with various persecutions at the time of the Reformation, such as the arrival of the Huguenots. In Camberwell, at Myatts Fields, a conservation area, a nineteenth-century estate around a park was built by a Huguenot refugee family that had prospered.

Ethnic minorities have been present in London since at least Roman times. The modern wave of migration of ethnic minorities is associated with the ship called the *Empire Windrush*, which in 1948 brought migrants from the Caribbean seeking employment.

Many Anglican churches had a poor record in welcoming these migrants. There were others that were quicker to embrace fellow Anglicans into their congregations, St Giles being one of them. During this period, St Giles was exploring how to encourage people to engage with one another, and set up house groups, but it was soon found that people in these groups had 'nothing more in common than a postcode', as the St Giles incumbent, Rodney Bomford, put it. Fr Bomford, schooled by Fr Diamond in Deptford, recognized that people might travel long distances to receive a welcome on a Sunday with the possibility of meeting people from their own particular cultural background, and he encouraged people from ethnic minorities to attend St Giles. Groups of people met from a variety of Caribbean islands. However, it wasn't until Isoline Russell was ordained an OLM in 2004 that this community was represented among the ordained leadership of the parish. Parishes such as St Giles have come a long way from the position where it would have been inconceivable to have a woman priest on the staff, to having three today; and from a position where ethnic minorities might be welcomed into a congregation, but not into the clerical caste.

Other communities, such as Cypriots, established themselves in the Camberwell area, particularly during the early postwar years. More recent waves of migration have been particularly associated with countries of West Africa, which is where Damilola Taylor's family came from. St Giles' changing congregation has reflected these migration waves, though the Cypriot community established their own Greek Orthodox Cathedral on the Camberwell New Road. (The church had formerly belonged to the charismatic Scottish nineteenth-century sect called the Catholic Apostolic Church.)

Changing educational climate

The early period saw education managed by the Inner London Education Authority (ILEA), which supplied a great variety of support services to schools in poorer communities. The ILEA was wound up in 1989 and education devolved to local authorities, with new arrangements for the local management of schools. All this was associated with more administration and the implementation of a national curriculum and associated testing. There was careful monitoring of primary and secondary schools in both the public and private sectors with OFSTED inspections. School and student performance was also monitored by the publication of league tables.

Education in inner areas of London suffered from increasing financial constraints, not just in investment in buildings and equipment, but also in terms of staffing. The profession haemorrhaged teachers. Some inner-city schools found it almost impossible to keep a teacher in front of every class. Gradually the situation eased. Headteachers became managerially and financially astute, and an ethos of striving for excellence accompanied the belief that every child could achieve. Sometimes 'failing' inner-city schools became beacon schools almost overnight. One such school in the Camberwell area was Archbishop Michael Ramsey Church of England secondary school which serves the parish of St Giles. A St Giles OLM is on the governing body.

Higher education is dealt with in Chapter 12, but one figure particularly important to the development of adult education in the Diocese of Southwark came from St Giles, Camberwell. Typical of a rather upper-class remnant in the parish was Dr Cecilia Goodenough (1905–98), grandchild of Lord Sheffield, the nineteenth-century liberal peer with a passion for the education of marginalized children. Like her grandfather, Cecilia was passionate about an instructed laity, and in the diocese was responsible for beginning the Southwark Pastoral Auxiliary (SPA) training course. She also worked for the Readers' course, was a theological trainer with the South London Industrial Mission (SLIM), and a member of the teaching staff of the Southwark Ordination Course as well as being Assistant Missioner in the diocese. Cecilia preached regularly at St Giles into her nineties and while she was in favour of the ordination of women, she neither saw it as something for herself nor became politically embroiled in the struggle for it.

2 The changing shape of the Church nationally: 1970–2005

Clergy and people

Half as many people attend a Church of England church now than did during the 1960s. Initially inner-city parishes suffered a worse decline, but recently South London has seen small increases. In the Camberwell deanery, for example, annual congregational counts suggest an increase over the period 1999–2002 of 10 per cent in adults and much the same among children.

There have been changes too in the deployment of clergy. At the beginning of the twentieth century there were about 29,000 stipendiary clergy in England. By 2005, this had dropped to 9,000. The last five years have seen clergy numbers declining faster than church membership, while numbers of church buildings have declined significantly less than both. The figures for the level of decline in 1990–5 are, respectively: stipendiary clergy down 17 per cent, Church membership down 9 per cent, and church buildings down 0.3 per cent.[2]

The deployment of clergy at St Giles has reflected this decline. Until 1986, St Giles had a full-time staff of up to three clergy most of the time (this included one curate responsible mainly for the daughter church of St Matthew, which was attached to the parish in about 1980). The rapid decline in clergy numbers during the 1990s led to a situation where at times there was only one priest in the parish, and for a parish used to a daily Mass this was a very difficult period.

The 'one man band' or 'Father knows best' style of leadership was coming under increasing pressure for a variety of reasons. Not least it put unrealistic pressure on stipendiary clergy who could not sustain the expectations of congregations and communities. Further, no one person possesses all the gifts required by a community of faith, and the talents of many laypeople were stifled. David Watson likened the situation to a 'bottleneck':

> Nothing can go in or out except through him. No meetings can take place unless he is the leader or chairman. No decisions can be made without his counsel or approach. This bottle concept of the church makes growth and maturing virtually impossible. Members are unable to develop into the God-given ministry they could well experience because, in structure and in practice, there is room for only one minister.[3]

While not suggesting any link between decline and particular issues facing the Anglican Church, one of the most divisive issues during the 1970s was the ordination of women. By 1984, the three houses of General Synod (bishops, clergy and laity) had agreed in principle to the ordination of women. In 1985 the Women Deacons Measure was passed, and from 1987 women could be ordained deacon on the same basis as men. In 1994 the first women were ordained priest, and nearly 100 were ordained in three groups in Southwark Cathedral at Petertide. In the Diocese of Southwark, some clergy and laypeople left the Church of England. A curate at St Matthew's, Camberwell, Fr Ashley Beck, left the Church of England to become a Roman Catholic.

Under Fr Rodney Bomford, St Giles had moved in a more Catholic direction, and it might have been expected that the ordination of women would be less likely than ever in such a parish. The reality was rather different. The incumbent's ill health was one of the reasons for the parish setting up a ministry team to assist in parish development. It was hoped that out of this team ordinands would emerge. The parish awayday at St Peter's, Vauxhall, produced two possible vocations to ordained ministry: both happened to be women. The result was that St Giles had its first woman priest in 2003, and its second and third in 2004. Two of the three are OLMs. The clergy staff is now mainly women and is back to the level it was at in the 1980s.

Church building

In the period 1969–84 the Church of England was declaring over 70 churches redundant annually. Camberwell's neighbouring Deanery of Brixton gives something of a picture of what the redundancy of church buildings means on the ground in an inner-city area. During the last 30 years, ten parishes originally making up the area that became the Brixton deanery (only a separate deanery because of the Brixton riots) have been reduced to seven, going on six. But that does not give half the story of the changes. One parish church became the proverbial furniture warehouse, and another was exchanged with the local Seventh Day Adventist Church for a smaller more manageable building. A third parish sold its church building to the New Testament Church of God and moved in with the Methodist Church. A fourth (a basilica purporting to be inspired by Hagia Sophia, Istanbul) was saved from redundancy by a small group of laity fighting closure all the way to the Privy Council and winning, which was a legal first! A fifth church, once the set for the TV series *O Brother*, became a housing co-operative. A sixth had a derelict chancel, separated from the working nave. (In 2004, the chancel was brought back into use as a nursery.) A seventh, one of the four churches commemorating the victory of Waterloo, was declared redundant, except for the narthex. This became the church area, while the rest of the building now houses a night club, bars and an entertainment complex. Only three churches in the deanery have remained substantially as built in the Victorian era: the Grade I listed church of St John the Divine, Kennington, designed by Edmund Street (though completely gutted in World War Two); St Michael's, Stockwell; and St Andrew's, Stockwell.

If Anglican churches were in difficulties, then it was much worse for the various mainline Free Churches in the inner city. In many areas they have almost disappeared. More than compensating for this decline, however, has been the enormous rise in the number of black-led churches, which either share buildings with other denominations (some Anglican churches have had as many as five other churches sharing their plant) or purchase their own buildings.

St Giles, one of Sir Gilbert Scott's architectural masterpieces, had weathered the storms of decay. During the incumbency of Fr Bomford, and with help from the Friends of St Giles, lottery funding, and assistance from other major trusts, this Grade II listed building has been restored. (During the restoration, £25,000 worth of gold Napoleonic francs appeared mysteriously in the church porch. They were unclaimed, and so after six months they became the parish's property.)

St Matthew's has also survived the threat of closure and now serves as an estate church staffed by St Giles clergy.

The changing economics of church life

Since the 1970s there has been a major shift in the economics associated with parish life. There has always been redistribution of wealth within the Church of England in order to support a parish system, and mainly to enable stipendiary ministers to be available throughout England, no matter how poor the community. Over the period 1970 to 2005, there have been a number of issues that have forced the Church as a whole to encourage congregations to give at ever more realistic levels so that such coverage can be maintained.

The stockmarket crash in October 1986 made it clear to the Church of England that it would be necessary to pay for ministry out of current giving rather than out of the dwindling historic assets of the Church. Then in 2001 there was a redistribution of the historic assets of the dioceses managed by the Church centrally, which placed an even greater burden on dioceses like Southwark, which found it necessary to reduce its budget. In 2002, the Diocese of Southwark needed to make cuts of £1.5 million in order to balance the budget. After wide consultation it was agreed to make a £1 million cut in the annual budget and to expect an increased contribution from parishes of £500,000. The Ordained Local Ministry Scheme, in the first round of the debate, was charged with becoming self-financing. The singling out of the Ordained Local Ministry Scheme in this manner was largely the result of misunderstandings about who was paying for what, and in the end all training courses within the diocese, including the Reader training course, the Southwark Pastoral Auxiliary training course and Certificate courses, were required to charge their students or their parishes, some for the first time.

The Southwark Diocesan 'Fairer Shares' scheme collects contributions from the parishes on the basis of agreed membership
figures and average member income. The scheme has the confidence of the parishes, and enables richer parishes to subsidize
poorer ones. The Parish of St Giles with St Matthew is a subsidized
parish. At St Giles, the congregation averages just over 100 on a
Sunday and makes a Fairer Shares contribution of £30,000 to the
diocese, while St Matthew's, with a congregation averaging 30 on a
Sunday, makes a Fairer Shares contribution of £5,500. The total
giving of the parish means that the diocese as a whole is subsidiz-
ing the two stipendiary clergy (incumbent and curate).

Moves towards inclusion

The ministry of Fr Rodney Bomford at St Giles (1977–2001) brought
with it a rather Catholic view of parish life. At the time of his
arrival, the Anglican Church was still struggling with its rather
austere 'Series 3' liturgy, and many priests of a Catholic disposition
in the Church of England tended to borrow from the new liturgical
material arising out of the Second Vatican Council (1962–5) which
began to be available from 1968. Bomford introduced use of the
Roman Catholic *Missa Normativa,* feeling that it offered greater
colour and drama in the liturgy, especially when accompanied by
Catholic ritual.

Fr Bomford also imported into St Giles a high doctrine of priesthood, which, while engaging with the local community, saw
ministerial relationships, at least initially, in terms of delegation.
Gradually delegation gave way to collaboration, and this change
can in large measure be associated with the development of
Ordained Local Ministry in the parish.

Another area of developing inclusion was in the area of race. The
McPherson Enquiry into the murder of Stephen Lawrence in 1993
was finally published in 1999, and it denounced 'institutional
racism'. The disquiet surrounding the investigation had deeply
exercised the Diocese of Southwark, with its enormous numbers
of church-going Christians from ethnic minorities. The report
challenged 'every institution to examine their policies and the
outcome of their policies and practices to guard against disadvantaging any section of our communities'. The Diocese of Southwark
was one of the first institutions, and certainly the first church institution, to take up the challenge. The Diocesan Synod, at the Bishop
of Southwark's request, commissioned Sir Herman Ouseley to produce a report (2000). The report made a number of recommendations relating to Ordained Local Ministry, and in particular asked

that vocations to ordained ministry should be encouraged among ethnic minorities. It also proposed three types of training ('anti-racist' training, 'cultural awareness' training, and 'empowerment' training for people from ethnic minorities). It also proposed the observance of Racial Justice Sunday and a greater awareness at every level of exclusion issues, from the preparation of mission statements and policies to practice on the ground. Progress in these areas has recently been reviewed in a follow-up report, which has been received by the Diocesan Synod. The *Review of Inclusive Ministry: Dealing with Institutional Racism* report (2005) begins by stating 'In an environment of social exclusion, racial and religious discrimination, and the continued marginalization of black and minority ethnic people in church and society, it is timely and perhaps prophetic that the Southwark Diocese of the Anglican Church has undertaken this Review.' The report sees the Church of England as having a distance to travel, but it also notes progress. Camberwell Deanery Synod, for example, almost doubled the number of representatives from ethnic minorities from 23 per cent to 54 per cent.

Inclusion in terms of women and race might be moving in a more positive direction, though with a distance to go in both cases; but in other areas of church life inclusion is felt by many to be going into reverse. The Gloucester report of 1979 concluded with rather open comments that there were 'circumstances in which individuals may justifiably choose to enter into a homosexual relationship with the hope of enjoying a companionship and physical expression of sexual love similar to that found in marriage'. There were a number of intervening comments and reports, which then led to the rather different comments of the 1998 Lambeth Conference which 'rejected all homosexual activity as incompatible with Scripture'.

Another field in which progress seems to have gone into reverse is the ecumenical movement. The ecumenical movement of the postwar period was beginning to run out of steam by the end of the 1970s. For example, the great optimism that envisaged the reunion of Methodist and Anglican Churches came to a crashing halt in 1969 when the Methodists accepted the proposals and the Anglicans rejected them. Meanwhile, dialogue was also taking place between two 'sister churches', the Roman Catholic and Anglican Churches, as a result of a meeting between Archbishop Ramsey and Pope Paul VI in Rome in 1966. The subsequent Anglican–Roman Catholic International Commission (ARCIC) reported on Eucharistic Doctrine (1971), on Ministry and Ordination (1973) and on Authority (1976): all evidence of great steps forward in shared understanding. In 1981 the final report was produced which sounded the rather optimistic note: 'There are high expectations that significant initiatives will be boldly undertaken to deepen our reconciliation and lead us forward in the quest for the full communion to which we have been committed, in obedience to God, from the beginning of our dialogue.' This was followed by the first papal visit in history to England. Despite the ARCIC report, which was finally accepted in 1985, and the papal visit to Canterbury Cathedral, like the Methodist/Anglican pilgrimage to union before it, the signs of impending reconciliation led to very little.

From maintenance to mission: the development of ministry teams

Over the period in question the Church has become more conscious of the need for a more missionary strategy. A falling membership and financial constraints were clearly important reasons. Another reason was the need to grapple with changing culture, especially in inner-city Britain. John Tiller's *Strategy for the Church's Ministry*[4] and *Faith in the City*[5] were published in the mid-1980s. These led many dioceses to look seriously at the areas of mission, ministry and training. In the mid-1980s the then Bishop of Southwark, Ronald Bowlby, set up a Ministry Development Group to follow through the policy issues raised during the debate on the Tiller report. Previous work within the diocese provided valuable background in this area, and reports such as *People and Places* (1979) and *The Shape of Ministry* (1983) were brought out of hibernation. The Ministry Development Group was chaired by the then Bishop of Woolwich, Peter Hall, and among its members was the late Mark Birchall who, together with John Tiller, had done a considerable amount of work researching developments in 'local' and 'collaborative' ministry. Thus it was in 1987 that this group presented a report to the Southwark Diocesan Synod which was unanimously accepted. The group recognized that a variety of informal ministry teams were springing up within the diocese, and one of their report's recommendations was that certain parishes should 'select a team for training for local ministry on the basis that some of the team may continue as lay members of the team with no formal title, some may become Readers or Pastoral Auxiliaries and some may be called in due course to a local non-stipendiary ministry'.

The diocese then appointed the Reverend Geoff Mason as Ministry Development Adviser to help implement the report's recommendations and work with the Development Group. Another appointment was that of Wendy Saunders as Urban Ministry Adviser, for it was apparent that the number of vocations from inner-city parishes was well below that in other areas of the diocese. There was also a need for training courses to encourage laypeople to develop their gifts and grow in confidence at parish level, and courses of various kinds were developed during the 1990s by Chris Chapman, Wendy's successor. Not all ministry teams flourished, and some proved ineffective or of limited life, but some nurtured vocations from inner-city parishes to different patterns of accredited ministry, and many people grew in confidence through the experience. The present Bishop of Southwark, Tom Butler, has given great impetus to the encouragement of vocations from minority ethnic people, who have made up at least 20 per cent of Ordained Local Ministry candidates in the past seven years.

St Giles, with the encouragement of Chris Chapman (lay training adviser to the diocese), set about establishing a ministry team, beginning with an awayday in Vauxhall. The day gathered together a group of about ten people, including the incumbent. The group was representative of the mix of racial groups in the congregation, and like the congregation it was predominantly composed of women. The group was commissioned in 1996 by the then Bishop of Woolwich, the Right Reverend Colin Buchanan. One of the potential ordinands within the group commenced training in 1999, followed by another a year later. The way the group has changed and developed indicates some of the issues associated with developing ministry in the inner city. The group was more active at some periods than at others, the level of activity depending on the input of key personnel. People came and went, reflecting the mobility of the community, though even today five of the original ten remain, including the two priests. To be effective a group like this really needs a facilitator. The lack of such a person meant that those exploring their vocations as OLMs in the group found themselves taking a lead.

The Decade of Evangelism

During the 1990s the Church of England participated in a 'Decade of Evangelism'. It was certainly the decade when a freer and more assertive evangelical flavour was finding its voice in the Church of England. This expansion might symbolically be associated with the Alpha course sponsored by Holy Trinity, Brompton, as well as with aspects of the charismatic movement. While of itself the decade of evangelism may not have achieved much, it represented a changing attitude within the Church of England generally, a change from 'maintenance' to 'mission'. In 2004, *Mission-shaped Church*[6] was published. This report began life with another title (which became its sub-title): 'church planting and fresh expressions of church in a changing context', which indicates the nature of its approach to mission. The continuing place of Ordained Local Ministry is an important part of the strategy. The *Faith in the City* report saw Ordained Local Ministry as

> deriving inevitably and naturally from what is meant by a fully local church which reflects the culture of its area. By this is meant an indigenous church open to God, to each other, to the neighbourhood, to the world, and able to understand the present and potential spirituality of the area. Such a church would derive its identity and shape from the people in a particular place working out a way of living faithfully and would take full account of local cultures as well as geography.[7]

Mission-shaped Church continues to see ministry emerging 'from below', and it sees the effectiveness of ministry and mission in the future depending on 'our ability to identify, train and authorize "local" ministers' in context.[8]

The Diocese of Southwark has produced a range of documents that have impinged on the changing context of mission over the years. In 1993, the report *Renewal for Mission* was launched. This contained a six-point strategy that aimed to develop the mission of the Church in a personal, local, flexible and radical way and with a commitment to work ecumenically. The report had a sense of realism about it in recognizing that 'with approximately 1.5% of the population belonging to an Anglican church we need to be realistic about the extent to which we can tackle problems that we see around us. The challenges of Gospel and Kingdom require us to seek growth in numbers as well as in depth, so that we can be more effective in every part of our Mission.' The report enabled discussions to take place within the diocese with the aim of re-envisioning the Church.

Renewal for Mission was followed in 1994 by the report *Working Together*, which guided diocesan thinking for the next five years. This was not a new policy document, but rather faced the harsh realities of falling numbers of stipendiary clergy and falling congregational numbers and asked that 'at every level we must shift from a primary concern with pastoring the faithful to a commitment to Mission'. There was to be 'a commitment to renewal and growth for all parishes'.⁹ The report envisaged a reduction in clergy numbers, and especially of inter-parochial clergy; the re-organization of diocesan boards; and the establishment of Area Mission Teams led by the Area Bishops. Within the fine print of the report there were a number of recommendations affecting Ordained Local Ministry. 'Ministry Development Adviser', 'Voca-tions Adviser' and 'Local Ministry Adviser' posts were lost, but at the same time Ordained Local Ministry was encouraged, as was the development of local ministry teams.

The report *Growing Together*, circulated in 1999, established diocesan priorities for the period 1999–2004, and aimed to build upon *Working Together*. The report 'asked parishes and deaneries for their views on encouraging vocations and how to make best use of the available clergy and lay people, on the deepening of discipleship and welcome of new members, and on what advisory services they had found helpful to fulfil their mission'.

The parish of St Giles' attitude to mission over the period has been interesting. In the early period, under the incumbency of Douglas Rhymes (1970–6), the emphasis seems to have been on developing the congregation through lay training in order to develop mission. Some outward manifestations of this mission were the development of a Credit Union and the St Giles Home-lessness Project, both still active today. The building and plant of the parish were seen as something of a hindrance to mission.

During the incumbency of Fr Bomford (1976–2001), there was a new focus. Here the building was seen not only as necessary, but also as capable of making 'a powerful public statement of the Church's presence'. The buildings became tools of mission, mak-ing it important to refurbish some of the buildings for secular use and to restore the magnificent Gothic church building as a place for the gathered people of God to celebrate the liturgy. The liturgy became *the* missionary activity, supplemented with engagement with the community – for example, through the Camberwell Choir School and the jazz club. This policy has continued.

Conclusion

The period 1970–2005, hardly more than a third of a century, has seen massive changes in Church and society. No part of Britain has escaped the process, though Camberwell in the inner city of a rapidly developing global capital, with the Canary Wharf complex now visible as a backcloth, has seen changes more radical than many. The church community of St Giles with St Matthew, Camberwell, has sought to be open to the voice of God in the current age. In 1970 it would have been inconceivable that two women from the congregation, one born and bred locally and the other an immigrant from Jamaica, would be active priests within the congregation, helping to sustain and develop the life of the parish. If we think ourselves forwards 30 years from now, what might we find that would be inconceivable to us today? We need to be open to unexpected new possibilities in changes ahead.

Further reading

Hastings, Adrian, *A History of English Christianity 1920–1990*, 3rd edn, SCM Press, London, 1991.

Hurst, Antony, *The Diocese of Southwark 1905–2005: A Centennial Celebration*, Diocese of Southwark, London, 2004.

Faith in the City: The Report of the Archbishop's Commission on Urban Priority Areas, Church House Publishing, London, 1985.

Notes

1 Hastings, Adrian, *A History of English Christianity 1920–1990*, 3rd edn, SCM Press, London, 1991, p. 600.

2 Brierley, Peter (ed.), *UK Christian Handbook: Religious Trends No. 4, 2003/2004*, Christian Research, London, 2003, p. 8.2.

3 Watson, David, *I Believe in the Church*, Hodder & Stoughton, London, 1978.

4 Tiller, John, *A Strategy for the Church's Ministry*, Church Information Office, London, 1983.

5 *Faith in the City: The Report of the Archbishop's Commission on Urban Priority Areas*, Church House Publishing, London, 1985.

6 Archbishops' Council, *Mission-shaped Church: Church Planting and Fresh Expressions of Church in a Changing Context*, Church House Publishing, London, 2004.

7 *Faith in the City*, p. 112, para. 6.35.

8 Archbishops' Council, *Mission-Shaped Church*, p. 135.

9 *Working Together*, Diocese of Southwark, London, 1999, pp. 3–4.

5. A Working Party is Formed

STEPHEN LYON

> Select from among yourselves seven . . . full of the Holy Spirit and of wisdom, whom we may appoint to this task. (Acts 6.3)

The first time I heard about Ordained Local Ministry was when I received a letter from the then Bishop of Woolwich, Peter Hall, inviting me to join a working party: a working party that had been charged with the task of creating a scheme for training OLMs in the Diocese of Southwark. At the time I was the incumbent of a large parish in Kingston upon Thames, came from an open evangelical background, and had expressed on a number of occasions the need to offer rigorous training to those in local leadership. So with little knowledge of what lay ahead over the 18 months it would take to construct the Scheme, or of the background that led to this invitation, I agreed to join the working party and attended my first meeting.

Two things became immediately clear. The first was that this proposed Scheme was part of a movement of ministerial thought and experiment that had a significant history. The second was that the timing of this venture in Southwark was crucial as it enabled at least three significant people to join that working party.

Tiller and *Faith in the City*

This book has already outlined how experiments in Bethnal Green, Brandon and Bermondsey had taken seriously the assumption that within each locality, whatever its social status, there were those deeply rooted in their communities who could, with the right pattern of training, exercise an ordained ministry *within that locality*. These experiments were part of Southwark's history, but they were just that: experiments. The next step had to be to regularize these 'different approaches' so that they could be seen by the Church as normal and therefore acceptable.

The experiments were not without their admirers in nationally influential positions. In 1983 John Tiller, then Chief Selection Secretary of the Advisory Council for the Church's Ministry (ACCM), was commissioned to write a report on the future of ordained ministry within the Church of England. The Tiller Report,[1] as it became known, offered a theological and practical case for what is now Ordained Local Ministry. While Tiller did not give this form of ministry this title or see it as the departure from the norm that some accused Ordained Local Ministry of being, he nevertheless saw it as a part of the Church of England's ministerial future. It could be said, in retrospect, that the Tiller Report was too far ahead of its time to be treated with the seriousness it deserved. For those with ears to hear, it spoke volumes.

The other publication that gave support to the concepts behind Ordained Local Ministry was *Faith in the City*.[2] This report saw the need for a more indigenous leadership within our urban churches, and Ordained Local Ministry as one of the answers. Bethnal Green was held up as a possible model but more work was needed to ensure that such a form of ministry was rigorously prepared for and carefully thought through by those embarking on it.

Southwark Diocese took both reports seriously and had done considerable work in encouraging parishes to identify key lay-people who, together with the ordained staff, could form a ministry team to provide collaborative leadership and ministry. Not surprisingly, the next question that would arise, especially because of the experiments in Bethnal Green, Bermondsey and the Brandon Area, was 'Why not ordination?' So by unanimous agreement the Diocesan Synod passed the resolution that set up the working party I had been invited to join.

Three significant figures

It was very clear that the working party had to evaluate past experiments and other similar developments in Lincoln and Manchester, ensure that there was a sound theological and educational basis that could meet the challenge such a Scheme presented, and finally put it all together in a way that would win the approval of the House of Bishops. So it was crucially important that the membership of the working party could deliver in all of these areas.

Professor Walter James was just about to retire as Professor of Education at the Open University. He lived in Blackheath, was known within the diocese, but was about to move to the south coast. Walter would be able to offer a great deal to our explorations of the educational approach of the Scheme and might even be persuaded to chair the whole venture. Like many 'about to be retired' people, he was reluctant to take on fresh responsibilities, especially as he was moving out of the diocese. Peter Hall was never someone to let such practicalities get in the way of a good catch, so he dispatched Geoff Mason, the Diocesan Ministry Development Officer, to persuade Walter to take on this task. He succeeded.

Hilary Ineson had recently started work as an adult education adviser at the Board of Education at Church House in Westminster. As with most recently appointees, Hilary's diary had an early flexibility that allowed her to accept the invitation to join in this venture. Not only did Hilary bring her adult education skills to bear, but prior to coming to London she had worked in Manchester and was heavily involved in designing their Ordained Local Ministry Scheme.

Ted Roberts was serving in the Southwark Diocese, but due to health problems was no longer working in a parish full time. However, with his health improving Ted wanted to increase his involvement in the life of the diocese, and he also accepted Peter Hall's invitation to join the working party.

So as we gathered for that first meeting we had a group of people who held between them a quite remarkable set of skills, experiences and knowledge about the task in hand. It contained an ex-Professor of Education who, as a result of retirement, had time enough to chair the group and also to write the first drafts of much of the final document. We had another educationalist who had worked closely on a Scheme in a diocese with many of the same characteristics as Southwark. We had the only person within the Church of England (possibly the Anglican Communion) who had selected, trained and worked with OLMs in two different settings. Finally, we had a number of other people who between them brought rich resources of theological understanding, wide parish experience and adult educational practice.

Accreditation – aiming for permanence

The completion of the accreditation document coincided with a period of financial stringency within the diocese. This meant that there was no guarantee that even if the House of Bishops gave the Scheme its blessing, the diocese could afford it. A freeze had been placed on beginning any new areas of work that would have signif- icant financial implications for an overstretched budget. It was estimated that with salary and training expenses the Scheme would cost in the region of £64,000 for its first three years of operation.

The kind offices of the City Parochial Foundation, who offered a grant to fund the first three years of the Scheme, solved the immediate financial problem. Without this grant it is likely that the Scheme, which had been given the House of Bishops' approval in January 1992, would have been shelved at birth. While those of us who had worked on the Scheme were delighted by this generous response, it did possibly give rise to an issue that would have to be dealt with later – that is, how do you ensure that the diocese *owns* the Scheme?

In the light of this funding, Bishop's Council gave the Scheme the green light in the spring of 1992. But it was not until 1995 that the diocese had to take on any financial responsibility for the Scheme. In one sense the timing was good as diocesan funding started in the year the first intake of candidates were due to be ordained. However, if we show the value of something by our willingness to pay for it, then the diocese was getting a Scheme it had to make little initial financial investment in. Be that as it may, by the late spring of 1992 Southwark had an officially recognized Ordained Local Ministry Scheme; all it needed now was a Principal and some ordinands to train.

A Principal and its first ordinands

The question of the Principal was dealt with speedily. The post was advertised and a shortlist of one was drawn up. An interview lasting an hour and three-quarters followed and, after much deliberation, the appointment was made. Once I was appointed it was my task, with the help of many others, to turn a document into reality.

However, there was still the question of candidates to train. Ordained Local Ministry was new, not only for the diocese, but also for the wider Church. So what kind of process do you use to select ordinands for a ministry that, in some respects, is distinctively different from the inherited models, yet stands, in other respects, in the same line? The answer lay in holding both the *local* and the *universal* (or national) together in selection. So in the summer of 1992 the Advisory Board for Ministry (ABM) held the first Southwark Selection Conference using national criteria and Bishops' Selectors from both inside and outside the diocese. The end result was that seven candidates – the 'guinea pigs', as they named themselves – were recommended for training, and in

September the Southwark Ordained Local Ministry Scheme was up and running.

The training programme

The ethos of the training programme can be summed up as follows:

- It was to be *grounded in the local*. All that we did on the Scheme was referenced back to the differing 'locals' of each candidate.
- It was based around *five central themes* of theological knowledge and understanding that seemed vital for candidates to have in order to exercise a Local Ordained Ministry. These were an understanding of the communal or corporate; of the individual; of the Church; of the world with which that Church engages; and of spirituality and spiritual growth. (Later, a sixth theme, 'an understanding of the faith we inherit', was added.)

  These themes also illustrate the way in which the educational model sought constantly to integrate theory and practice in every aspect of the training.
- It was to have a *collaborative educational style* based around the small training year group, the whole Scheme group, and the support group within the local parish setting.

The accreditation document had planned the teaching programme for Year 1 in considerable detail while only offering the outline for Years 2 and 3. These were to be worked up during the first 12 months of the Scheme. This felt an extremely creative process as we could learn from how things were progressing, experiment without being held to account too soon, and try out innovative possibilities with the freedom to fail as well as succeed. But we were also conscious of the fact that this was no longer 'experimental'; it was to become a permanent feature not only in Southwark's landscape but also in the Church of England's landscape. Looking back, we were probably less innovative than we thought we were, but we did have the space and freedom to do things differently, and to some extent we did that.

Important foundations

In seeking to roll out the course, we put in place a number of key structural features that provided the framework for the new scheme. The first was the emphasis we laid on the Scheme's staff getting to know the different *locals* represented on the Scheme. Having just moved out of a busy parish, and with only seven candidates to look after in the first year, my diary was not over-full. Unused to such a luxury, I suggested to the incumbents of those in training that I spend a day with them in their parishes, returning on the Sunday to preach or preside at their main act of worship. I was amazed at how these visits transformed my perception of what the candidates were doing in training. Instead of seeing seven individuals, I saw seven communities seeking, through their candidate, to discern what co-operating in God's mission meant for them. It also enabled us to build strong relationships with one of the key players in the training venture, the candidate's incumbent. This paid dividends if, in later months, we hit difficulties that required hard pastoral decisions to be made. This pattern of visits continued as new candidates joined each year.

The second feature was the emphasis we laid on the practical and pastoral placements candidates undertook each year. However, we realized that if we were to make the most of these experiences, then more help was needed in setting them up, preparing the candidates adequately, supervising and debriefing the placement, and marking the final reflective report. The problem was solved by Judith Roberts moving into the diocese with not only the skills to undertake all these tasks, but also the time to become an indispensable part of the core staff. Judith's importance was recognized by the support that a subsequent inspection gave for the application to make her appointment permanent and paid.

Over the first five years of the Scheme's life, Judith developed the placements during each of the three years, together with all the preparatory materials and debriefing processes. The first year's placement was within a voluntary organization within the candidate's own community. This provided an opportunity to deepen the candidate's involvement and knowledge of what others in their area were doing. The second year's placement was at a church 'of a different tradition' to their own. For many candidates their rootedness within their own community meant they had seldom had the opportunity to worship with any regularity in another church. The third year's placement enabled the candidates to experience ministry in a context outside the parish in a hospital, prison, school, airport or a variety of other settings.

The third key structural feature we established in the early years of the Scheme was a strong and challenging pastoral relationship with a clergyperson. These pastoral relationships played an important role in either pushing the candidates beyond their own com-

fort zones or, if this was done by the course itself, journeying with
them to try to help them make sense of the situation. We asked
these tutors to meet each year with the Scheme's staff, to take part
in the annual assessment process, and to be available for regular
meetings with the candidates. While not every pastoral tutor/
candidate relationship achieved all we hoped for, most did, and
they played a significant part in the transformational process
towards ordination.

The first years

Life for the 'guinea pigs' had sufficient pre-planned elements
to give it a sense of direction and purpose, but there were also a
number of gaps that could only be filled in as we went along. At
times these gaps were unexpected, such as a large one that
appeared on the first evening session in September 1992.

The first module was to be an analysis of a parish audit or profile
that all candidates assured me their parish had undertaken. Within
20 minutes of the first session beginning, it was clear that what
candidates brought with them was not what we had anticipated.
Yes, they all had something that resembled a parish audit or
profile, but some were a few years out of date, some candidates
had little or nothing to do with their audit so could not easily
explain how conclusions were reached, and all were written for
different reasons, none of which was to do with ordination training. The brave new world of Ordained Local Ministry training felt
a little frail at the end of session one. However, Liz Gould and Ann
Stricklen (two former diocesan employees) skilfully redeemed the
situation in time for session two by constructing a simple, effective
and sufficiently comprehensive audit checklist to enable the candidates to map and analyse the significant features of their locality.

This process of seeming failure followed by redemption was a
common feature in the first few years of the Scheme. The only
group of candidates that did not directly benefit from this process,
in the sense that it enabled us to get it 'more right' for the next
group, were the 'guinea pigs'. While the next few intakes also
struggled with these creative changes, the 'guinea pigs' bore the
brunt of them, with remarkable fortitude, but they did so not as
uninvolved victims but as participants in this creative process.
They were the group who scored highest on the average age
scale, but that maturity meant that they brought considerable
experience into the training arena. For example, a retired headteacher, a retired senior police officer, a retired buyer for a large

national DIY chain and an engineer coping with long-term unemployment had considerable experience to bring to this venture, and they drew on it for themselves and for others. They were prepared to fail, prepared to let go of things that were not working, prepared to keep going in case it did work, and prepared to laugh at both success and failure.

Like a parent with their first child, I was aware of the flood of mixed emotions that we would experience when the second training group joined the Scheme in 1993. This was a group very different from the 'guinea pigs' – younger, more women, most at work and, like all the groups I was privileged to work with, unique! Another group of seven candidates, all with vast experience of life, ministry and mission and willing to throw themselves into this partially formed training venture. In September 1994 a further five candidates started training and for the first time we had a full Scheme, although there was still no fruit to show for all our efforts in terms of dog collars.

The first end-products

This happened in the following September when for the first time those joining the Scheme saw at their first residential weekend that people did leave and would get ordained. But the question arose as to how you marked the end of training in a way that rightly acknowledged the achievements of the past three years but appropriately complemented the cathedral ordination service. The answer was the annual Thanksgiving Service.

Each group of candidates was to be asked to design their own service that would take place at Wychcroft, the diocesan retreat house used for our residential weekends. The event would be on the Saturday afternoon of the September residential, and about a fortnight before their ordination. We gave them a few guidelines to ensure that it did not challenge the ordination service: for instance, that it had to be a service that they designed together, it had to be non-Eucharistic, and there were to be no bishops in sight. (We had to relax this stipulation when Bishop Colin Buchanan became the third Chair of the Ordained Local Ministry Council and had to be there to present the certificates.) These services became memorable occasions of worshipful thanks for what had happened over the previous three years. They also acted as an annual encouragement that there was an end point to the training process.

An early tension

There was, however, one noticeable tension in the Scheme over its early years. That was the struggle between the vision out of which Ordained Local Ministry grew – collaborative ministry in a local setting – and the pragmatic choices needed to ensure that the Scheme continued to survive. Within the first few years of the life of the Southwark Scheme, a number of other dioceses were exploring Ordained Local Ministry. One of the questions we all needed to ask was: How do you gauge whether a parish (and especially its incumbent) is actively promoting and exercising a collaborative ministry? No incumbent interested in Ordained Local Ministry is going to answer the question 'Are you?' in the negative.

In many dioceses the answer was 'because they have a ministry team' and often '. . . of the kind specified by the diocese'. But while Southwark was encouraging parish development through the establishment of ministry teams (and not only for the purposes of training an OLM), we did not specify what a team should look like. So many models of ministry team were produced as evidence of collaborative ministry – leadership teams, clergy/reader teams, the PCC, parish group leaders meeting, and so on. However, if we pushed this point too hard, insisting that some parishes wait until such a team was properly developed, we would have suffered from a severe lack of possible candidates for training. So the pragmatic choice was made that teams would follow candidates if necessary.

Theological and ecclesiological purists may feel that this was a cop-out. My own view was that all our ministry and mission is the art of seeking God's grace to redeem the possible and of making the most of the opportunities this presents. Looking back, possibly with somewhat rose-tinted spectacles, I believe that in most cases we did just that. However, there was one particular set of circumstances where I believe this policy created its own problems.

This was the situation where there was an interregnum in a parish with an OLM in place, but without a securely defined structure of collaborative ministry. The tendency, especially if the OLM had been priested, was for the lot to fall on the OLM – and often this was quite a lot. A number of OLMs were flattered by such responsibilities, and initially colluded with the parish's (and diocese's) expectations and projections, only to find the pressure too much after a few months of interregnum. It was then necessary to initiate restorative work to enable the vision of collaboration to be worked out more practically in the hope that the new incumbent would build on these foundations.

The first inspection and re-accreditation

In 1996 the Southwark Scheme underwent its first inspection. This process, one that all theological training courses go through every five years, was going to provide a rigorous benchmark for the quality of the Scheme after its initial period of operation. It would also provide the basis upon which the second accreditation process would be built.

The preparatory paperwork for an inspection is considerable, but it did provide evidence of some of the obvious strengths of the Scheme. For example, we were required to list all the Scheme's course tutors. The teaching programme was split into three- or four-week modules with, on average, four modules making up each of the two-term Study Courses. Each module had a separate tutor, which meant that candidates were taught by approximately two dozen people throughout their three years. Southwark could boast of a 'faculty' second to none in that we drew on at least three retired theological college principals, numerous theological college and university lecturers, all Southwark's bishops, a group of highly qualified adult educators, some expert social and development workers, and the recently retired Professor of Adult Education at the Open University. Many of those involved in the teaching were now serving in parishes and were eager to combine their past life in academia with their present pastoral role for the benefit of future ministry.

It was also clear from our inspection paperwork that the governance of the Scheme was instrumental in laying its initial foundations. In the first ten years the Council had three distinguished Chairs – Walter James, Martin Baddeley (who had been Principal of the Southwark Ordination Course (SOC), but was by then Archdeacon of Reigate), and Colin Buchanan, Bishop of Woolwich, but in a previous life Principal of St Johns Theological College in Nottingham. The Council's mandate was to provide rigorous oversight of the Scheme by representatives of all its stakeholders (candidates, incumbents, the wider diocese and the wider Church). (There was also a Board of Studies, charged with developing the programme and reviewing modules after they'd been taught, and the Board's Chair was also a member of the Council.) The Council's deliberations in the first six years provided a useful platform for the inspection process.

The inspection took place over a seven-month period in 1996–7. The three inspectors were Canon Ronald Coppin, then a Residentiary Canon at Durham Cathedral and Chairman of the House of Bishops' Committee on Inspections; the Reverend David Peacock, then Principal of Whitelands College; and the Reverend June Winfield, a former Industrial Chaplain in the London Diocese.

The basic question the inspectors were seeking to answer was 'Is this Scheme delivering what it outlined in its first accreditation document?' The inspectors met individuals and groups (the Diocesan Bishop, the Council, the Pastoral Tutors) and observed evening teaching sessions, weekends and a Study Day. They did this with remarkable sensitivity and thoroughness and became part of the scenery for almost two terms. At the end of the process they prepared their report and allowed me as Principal to see it in draft form and to challenge anything within it that I thought was unfair, and then they wrote the final version for the House of Bishops.

The report and its recommendations

The report contained a number of recommendations, many of which had already become part of the ongoing conversations during the inspection process. One was that we review the role and composition of the Council to clarify and strengthen its work. The report also recommended a number of measures to further strengthen the pastoral support of candidates and to offer them personal space in the midst of their training. It also requested that we review the way we debriefed placements and marked work, seeking a greater robustness in both. But there were three other significant areas in the report that merit longer comment.

The first was not a formal recommendation, because the inspectors had no authority to make it one, but it was an offer of strong support for making Judith's position, as Vice-Principal and Placements Tutor, a 'recognized, paid half-time' post. The inspectors' reasoning was not that the Scheme needed more time from Judith, but that the diocese should express its ownership of and commitment to the Scheme by providing adequate staffing levels. The Bishop's Council, when it came to discuss the inspection report, readily agreed to this suggestion.

The second significant area went to the very heart of Ordained Local Ministry. It was a recommendation that we strengthen the opportunities that a candidate's parish might have to participate in the training process. It came from the inspectors' desire to see us put a greater focus on collaborative training *within the parish context* as an important expression of a collaborative ministry. We addressed this by identifying a number of modules and assignments that candidates could undertake with a group from the parish.

Doctrinally and biblically light?

The third and most contentious recommendation was one the inspectors made concerning the content of the teaching programme. During the inspection, questions were raised about what they saw as a low level of explicit biblical and doctrinal content in the programme. They acknowledged that by taking the thematic approach we would not have specific modules on Old Testament, New Testament, salvation, the person of Christ, etc., and that a considerable amount of the content of each of the course's subject areas explored biblical and doctrinal themes. However, they questioned whether it was sufficiently explicit and whether it was enough. This led to some interesting discussion with the inspectors on how, for example, we would know whether an Ordained Local Ministry candidate knew the meaning of Christmas. My response was that they may not be able to write a 3,000-word essay on 'The Meaning of the Incarnation in the late Twentieth Century', but that they would be equipped to speak at a school carol service or care for an elderly parishioner about to spend her first Christmas as a widow after 40 years of marriage.

The recommendation itself was that 'the Scheme should define a core body of theological knowledge and understanding for its ordinands and indicate how and where within the context of training such knowledge and understanding are to be acquired' (Recommendation 4d). The Council had to respond to the inspection report and in relation to this, they said:

> of all the recommendations . . . this one caused the most discussion and concern. The Council acknowledged the reasons for [it] and the relative ease with which such a definition could be provided. However, the request . . . flies in the face of our basic approach. The Scheme, by its very design, has deliberately sought to integrate the acquisition of theological understanding and knowledge with ministerial and personal development. To extract from such a programme the 'core body of theological knowledge and understanding' appears at odds with such an approach. While such a body could be defined and, if seen as efficacious, be included within our new [accreditation] document, we would value further discussions on the matter.[3]

This discussion was ongoing both with the inspectors and, more importantly, with those deployed by The Advisory Board of Ministry to scrutinize and finally recommend our new accreditation document.

Overall, the inspection report marked a watershed for the Scheme. The inspectors were 'greatly impressed by the Scheme' and acknowledged its success. But they also saw an opportunity, through the inspection, to 'encourage and build on the strengths, as well as to consider how the weaknesses may be diminished', so that the Scheme could 'provide an even better training'. When the Bishop's Council came to discuss the report they accepted its recommendations, and their wholehearted agreement to fund the half-time post for Judith did, as the report suggested, show 'a recognition of the place which the Scheme has in the ministerial training provision of the Diocese'. The Scheme had truly become Southwark's – owned, affirmed and financed by the diocese.

The next phase

While this was a huge vote of confidence for all that we had achieved since the working party was set up in 1990, the inspection report, and especially recommendation 4d, left me with concerns about its future. We were now mainstream, at least within Southwark, but were we in danger of losing the vision that had started in Bethnal Green with Ted Roberts, and was the Scheme becoming institutionalized?

The outcome of Recommendation 4d was that a new Study Course was added to the training programme in the unfinished re-accreditation document I left for my successors. It had clear and explicit biblical and doctrinal modules that we attempted to incorporate into the ethos of the Scheme in terms of their delivery (parts were explored in parish groups) and its assessment (a multi-section assessment with a 'theory' and an 'applied pastoral' section). But the process towards re-accreditation was one I found laborious and difficult. On reflection now, almost five years after leaving the Scheme, there were probably two reasons for these feelings. It was laborious because the process of writing an accreditation document is hard work. It is almost an art form in itself because its language needed a particular kind of precision that sometimes seemed to have little to do with the regular engagement I had with the ordinands in training. It was difficult because I was continually aware that every time we put something new into the Scheme we squeezed a little more of the 'space' we had created out of it. There would be less room to linger over or enjoy exploring a topic. It was becoming less forgiving, and more demanding, of the time that was available.

It was during this process that I moved on from the Scheme, and although grappling with the re-accreditation was not the reason for my move, it was the one bit of the job that I did not miss!

So what did I feel was at stake? In a nutshell, was the Scheme becoming too academic, in the wrong sense of the word? In the sense that it might bar from training those with a clear giftedness for and call to Ordained Local Ministry because they lacked a high enough standard of formal education? My greatest delight and sense of achievement was seeing those who, in the past, would not have been trained as clergy due to their educational and/or ethnic background, flourishing in the training environment (often with a huge struggle) and then, more importantly, exercising a highly effective ordained ministry.

Would we lose that in our re-accreditation, and would we lose it with external validation? These were both questions I left un-answered and that Nigel Godfrey, my successor as Principal, and Judith Roberts had to take forward. The answer, I am sure, is not an inevitable 'yes', but it felt a little harder to ensure that it wouldn't be 'no'.

Further reading

Tiller, John, *A Strategy for the Church's Ministry*, Church Information Office, London, 1983.

Faith in the City: The Report of the Archbishop's Commission on Urban Priority Areas, Church House Publishing, London, 1985.

Stranger in the Wings: A Report on Local Non-Stipendiary Ministry, Advisory Board of Ministry Policy Paper no.8, Church House Publishing, London, 1998.

Notes

1 Tiller, John, *A Strategy for the Church's Ministry*, Church Information Office, London, 1983.

2 *Faith in the City: The Report of the Archbishop's Commission on Urban Priority Areas*, Church House Publishing, London, 1985.

3 'OLM Council response to the report of the Bishops' Inspection, for the Bishop's Council', 1997.

6. Pioneers Together

ARTHUR OBIORA

I am reminded of your sincere faith, a faith that lived first in your grandmother Lois and your mother Eunice and now, I am sure, lives in you. For this reason I remind you to rekindle the gift of God that is within you through the laying on of my hands; for God did not give us a spirit of cowardice, but rather a spirit of power and of love and of self-discipline. (2 Timothy 1.5–7)

A new scheme

When the Southwark Diocesan Ordained Local Ministry Training Scheme started in 1990, it was the Right Reverend Peter Hall, who was Bishop of Woolwich at the time, who said, 'It is no new thing to call people out from a local Christian community, to ordain them for ministry, and ask them to work in the local community which has called them.'

There may be some truth in what he said, but it was new to us; and after the Scheme had been explained to us one night at a PCC meeting, it slowly dawned on me what was really happening. If we took part in this radical new vision for ordained ministry, then we would be its pioneers. What we could never have known then was how our pioneering would leave the face of local ministry looking nearly ten years later.

The parish I live in and the church community I have grown up in and now serve as a priest is that of St Catherine's, Hatcham, at New Cross in South London. It is an exciting and challenging community, ethnically diverse and multicultural. The housing is still mainly made up of large Victorian dwellings, which are a reminder of a prosperous bygone era when this part of London was one of the many villages that surrounded the city. Now there is prosperity of a different kind. The growth of population and its international look have led to a demand for more housing and have seen the area grow as a place embracing difference. Many of these dwellings have been turned into flats. Some are privately rented, some are rented from the local authority or a housing association, and some are owner occupied.

The parish church had for many years been involved in its community, and in the late 1960s had built one of the first church-linked community centres, the Telegraph Hill Centre. But this was just one sign of the local church's preparedness to share more widely from its supply of gifts and resources, for there was already a tradition of shared ministry in the worshipping community. In St Catherine's, people were already discovering their gifts and using them for worship, mission and shared decision-making.

What was happening now was that we were being asked to consider taking part in a new Scheme – 'Ordained Local Ministry' – the idea being that someone from the parish and the local church community should be selected for training, trained largely in the parish, and ordained to serve in the parish.

Selection

I was already a Reader in the Church of England, and so I had some experience of preaching and leading worship, but I had been wondering about training for ordination for a while. However, having a young family and being rooted in London meant full-time residential training was not an option. The new Scheme seemed designed for my situation. I could respond to what I felt to be God's call, make a commitment to serve the church where I was without having unnecessarily to disturb my growing family in the security of home life. So I went to see Canon David Painter, who was then the Director of Ordinands for the Diocese of Southwark. We spent much of the time talking about Nigeria where he had accompanied, as his chaplain, the Most Reverend Donald Coggan, when he had been Archbishop of Canterbury. We talked about my childhood in Zaria in Northern Nigeria, and the fact that as a child Archbishop Fisher had visited our home. My father was himself a pioneer, for he had bought land in the area so that a church could be built.

After this interview, I followed the usual selection procedures adopted by the diocese and eventually was called to a full Selection Conference – a pioneering moment for the selectors as well as for us. The Selection Conference was only for candidates for Southwark's new Scheme and the selectors didn't seem to be entirely sure what they were looking for! This was hardly surprising since they were used to selecting for a ministry with an academic training, a ministry within which people would expect to move from one parish to another. The main problem as far as I could see was that we had been told that our parishes were being selected, along with ourselves, but there were no representatives of our parishes at the conference, which perhaps there really ought to have been.

The training

Most of us were selected for training, and the course began. Many of the tasks had to be completed in co-operation with representatives of the parish and church communities and this was evident from the start, for our first task was to create a neighbourhood profile. At St Catherine's, we had recently finished a parish audit, so it felt like we were half-way there from the outset; but it still required a lot of effort, and I was glad, for the extra work was rewarding and educational, and it made me get to know parts of the parish that I didn't know very well. But the rules of engagement didn't always seem very clear, and some of the candidates and their parishes struggled to complete the profile. One of the costs of being a pioneer is the frustration experienced when things like this happen and tasks are not made clear in advance. Having said that, I would also want to say that one of the positive elements to experiences like these was in knowing that the insights we fed back and the suggestions we made would make it better for those who would follow.

Among everyone concerned there was a sense of doing something new, and the course's Principal, the Reverend Stephen Lyon, often referred to the fact that we were all learning together – him included. One of the exciting aspects was that *everything* was new. The talks we heard and the exercises we took part in had never been done before in that place, in that way, and for that purpose. I can still remember some of the guest lecturers' talks, and the diagrams they used. I can also remember the arguments we had, particularly over how Christians should relate to other faiths. What I think I found particularly pleasing in the teaching sessions was the way in which our previous experience of life was valued. Somehow this matched up with the very core of what I think this kind of training does for us. It affirmed the value of life experience and helped us see how God had been working through our lives in everything to bring us to this moment of calling and decision.

Because the Scheme was new, our evening teaching sessions were a bit makeshift. The course took place in a converted church hall and we had to use someone else's office. Needless to say, it was very cramped as eight candidates, a Principal and a guest had to squeeze round a table, but we were soon allocated a larger space. At these evening sessions not only were we very aware that we were doing something new, for it was always practical, but the Bible was given serious study in order to inspire us to be good teachers, priests and pastors. I thought that Professor James's talks on the prophet Hosea were particularly inspirational.

At the heart of the course were the placements. Each year, for several weeks, we spent time in a situation that was new to us and from which we could learn the skills we'd need. My placements were in a local youth club, at Lewisham Hospital, and at St James's, Bermondsey – a church with a very different tradition from the one at St Catherine's. More than anything else it was these placements that taught me to be a priest. The youth club taught me how to relate to local young people and their culture (our own two children had been brought up very much in terms of our culture); the hospital taught me how to listen and how to pray with people in need; and St James's taught me how different Christians can be from one another.

An important element of the course was the work we did in peer groups. The year-group was divided into two peer groups. Some of our assignments were done in these groups, and the groups planned and led the worship. Working in groups is not always easy and some people find it particularly difficult, but things got a bit easier as more years were added to the Scheme, as then there were more groups to plan and lead worship on study days and at residential weekends. Something the Scheme didn't learn to do quickly enough was how to deal with personality clashes in such small groups. Another aspect that took a while to get right was the *pace* of the course. We were all in full-time jobs, and two of us had young children, and sometimes there was simply not enough time to complete assignments satisfactorily. We objected to what we sometimes regarded as harsh marking, particularly when we didn't think the markers had sufficient understanding of the nature and difficulty of the placements on which we were being evaluated.

I think that a course like this demands the best kind of leadership, and what made it all possible was the commitment and organizing ability of the Reverend Stephen Lyon, the Reverend Judith Roberts, our Vice-Principal, and Sue Maree, the course administrator. There were other things that marked it out as significant for me and introduced us to others in the diocese who were so supportive at every level: for example, something that really helped me was the annual retreat – particularly the one to which the Right Reverend Roy Williamson, Bishop of Southwark, attended. He gave us real encouragement.

What was also encouraging was the support we received from our parishes. Some of the assignments that were set by the course tutors had to be done with a group in the parish, and similarly when we had to preach in the parish we had to be marked on the sermon by people in the congregation. This was all new to the parish as well as to me, and we learnt together. Some of those who supported me during the training course still actively support me in my ministry, as does Father Graham Preston, who was my personal tutor during the course and is now my spiritual director.

A new kind of ministry?

The ordination as a deacon was emotional. People I had worked with in the Department of Work and Pensions came long distances to be present, and many people from the parish were there. Lots of people from the community came to the celebration afterwards at the Telegraph Hill Centre. I was quickly accepted as an ordained minister in the parish. Canon Francis Makambwe is the vicar and I am an OLM, but both of us are priests and we share presiding at the Eucharist equally.

There are certain frustrations that accompany this style of ordained ministry, but I tend to find that the frustrations are nothing to do with being an OLM – they are to do with not being as available as much as I would like to be. It is difficult for me to conduct funerals on weekdays, though when it's important that I be present for the funeral of a member of the congregation, I always try to take time off work.

This *is* a pioneering ministry, but in another sense it's simply the ministry of a priest in the parish, doing the kind of pastoral work that priests have always done.

Those who followed

In some ways, those who have followed our year group have had an easier time. There is more physical space in which to meet, there is a greater variety of placements, the course is more evenly paced, and the teaching is sometimes better. But they haven't experienced the same sense of being there first and of helping to create the Training Scheme and Ordained Local Ministry itself. To be one of the first representatives of Ordained Local Ministry in the diocese was both a responsibility and a privilege.

One of the important things that the course staff and ourselves established together was the centrality of the placements. Being a priest is expressed in the things that a priest does. The Scheme has changed and is changing still. However, I am convinced that whatever other changes occur, the placements should remain at the heart of the training.

The pioneers – Ken Gaved, Denis Hughes, Ray Ives, Dan Shackell, Hazel Kimber, Keith Sims and myself (and later Jack Lucas) – came from different backgrounds and parishes. The diocese is working hard to recruit people from different ethnic backgrounds and it must continue to work hard to recruit candidates from varied social backgrounds and different church traditions, for this diversity was one of the things that made our pioneering year so interesting.

New experience

I was grateful for the new experiences that the placements offered me, and when I look back on it now I think that the most formative part of the training course for me was the placement at the youth club in the parish, a club with people with special needs among its membership. What attracted me to this placement was the fact that I often shied away from youth clubs because I thought them associated with violence, and yet what I found particularly moving on this placement was the good relationship that existed between the young people with special needs and the other young people in the club. Lorraine Ferdinand, the senior youth worker, used her warm manner to handle difficult young people, and she made my relationship with the club easy from the start.

It was a culture shock for me (and really rather alarming) to discover how disruptive some of the young people could be. But Lorraine didn't seem to be at all concerned, and neither did her colleagues, Pamela, Stephen and Jackie. I was asked to look after the counter where sweets, drinks and biscuits were sold. Three particular girls made my life difficult (they would give me less money than they should have done, and they would try to steal things – or they would give me too much money to see what happened). Lorraine assured me that this was how they dealt with someone they cared about, and while I confess this took a little while to understand, eventually I warmed to them. Recently I baptized one of their daughters at St Catherine's, one of them is now a housing officer, and one is working in community care and is very involved in a Pentecostal church.

But the part of the experience that changed me most was caring for people with special needs: people who needed help with walking, drinking, or using the toilet. At the club they did exercises and meditation, led by able and kind-hearted Christine. Christine insisted that I should take part in everything the young people did and this brought me closer to them.

Human experience changes human attitudes, and what I am discovering is that just as these training experiences profoundly changed me, so the relatively new experience of Ordained Local Ministry is changing the Church's attitude to ordained ministry and its members' attitude to the Church. Someone has to be at the forefront of this new experience, and for me it was a privilege to be a pioneer in such an important new project.

7. Journeying Together in the Parish

EILEEN SERBUTT

. . . that by God's will I may come to you with joy and be refreshed in your company. (Romans 15.32)

I had attended the church of St Mary and St John the Divine, Balham, for some 30 years. I had been a PCC member, served as churchwarden for far too long, and trained as a Reader. During most of that time the church had been led by a lively but very traditionalist incumbent. When he eventually moved on and a young vicar, Theo Hull, was appointed, the culture changed. Women joined the choir and became servers, a young woman became a Reader, and we started to work together in groups formed for a particular purpose (for instance, a social committee), and a staff team began to meet regularly. Change came steadily, and by the time Dorothy Nicholson arrived as our next incumbent we had learned something about teamwork and shared ministry.

Dorothy formed a ministry team consisting of herself, two Readers, churchwardens, the minister for music, and the chairs of three committees of the PCC: Building and Finance, Congregation, and Mission. It was this ministry team that sent me forward, then supported me, during my selection process for the Ordained Local Ministry Training Scheme. The parish, by putting me forward as a candidate, had committed itself to developing further its pattern of collaborative learning and shared ministry.

Building a team

It was clear that the existing ministry team already had too many commitments and not enough time to support me through the training. They didn't want me to be just an item on a longer agenda, and they took seriously my need for support. The vicar and I drew up a list of people we could ask to form a support group. We wanted a group that knew both me and the church reasonably well, would be able to help and encourage me, provide resources, and act as a link with the PCC. They would also assist with reviewing and assessing my progress. We tried to select a balanced group representative of the congregation, though we found, as others have, that this is more or less impossible to achieve. Most of the people I approached agreed to join my support team (which for the rest of this chapter I shall call 'the team'); others could not commit themselves to the time involved, though they offered to assist when and where they could with specific, one-off tasks. The vicar decided she did not want to be in the group as she saw me regularly anyway. I was not very happy with this because I felt that I needed her experience and friendly encouragement at meetings, but it turned out to be a good decision as it gave me experience of leading people in new ways of approaching liturgy and of developing church educational programmes.

I had nine people in my team. Three were members of the congregation who had shown interest in the Ordained Local Ministry Scheme from the very beginning and saw membership of the team as a way to take further their own faith through working with me in the church. Two fellow choir members joined, as did a fairly new church member, a teenager, and a long-standing member of the church who had always been very supportive of my work. They all had very different skills and talents, and where we were lacking we could always call upon others to help.

Before retirement I had been headteacher of a large secondary school, so I had considerable experience of team management. At my first meeting with the team I set out to enable us to bond with each other and to lay down ground rules. We started with talk over wine and nibbles, then I explained what I had to do and how I hoped they could help. I stressed the importance of confidentiality. We decided on dates and times for meetings and quickly saw that not everyone could attend every meeting. Time was always going to be a problem and we had to recognize this from the start. Everyone was enthusiastic and wanted to stay in the group, so we allowed for occasional absence and I promised to keep everyone up to date. We organized two meetings a term and set agendas which consisted largely of allocating work, reviewing work and setting new targets.

Starting the journey

My first assignment was the Neighbourhood Profile. This was an excellent team-building exercise. It had to be done very quickly, mainly over August, as my Selection Conference only took place in July and so I was a late starter. However, my team provided ample data about health facilities, schools and local transport and helped me to devise a questionnaire for parishioners. I found an enthusiastic photographer in the congregation who really enjoyed being set loose with a camera in the area, and a local historian gave me maps and documents about Balham through the centuries. A computer expert analysed data collected and drew up charts and diagrams. She also organized material gathered from the questionnaire I gave to people about life in Balham generally and with regard to the church in particular.

The Neighbourhood Profile provided a specific task with a set outcome and my team (with co-opted members) produced a file of current data that I could use when I undertook other assignments later in the course. The profile was presented to the PCC and to the congregation as information that would be useful to all of us as we planned future development for the church. It was important for my team because it established clearly our position in the church. The team gained identity, and my own role as an OLM candidate was promoted.

From our work on the Profile we were able to begin to think about an action plan and the team saw that they could encourage other church members and groups to help in various ways. The team grew in confidence as they realized they could make things happen.

Change

Change came suddenly. A fire destroyed the baptistery and the narthex. When the cleaning up was over and the church reorganized to accommodate services and other usual activities, I sat down with my team to work out how we would be affected. They responded well. They recognized that I would need even more support to cope with assignments involving liturgy and setting up any new activity because now space and resources were limited.

During this time, two members of my team left the district. We did not replace them with permanent members, as we felt our group was strong enough to continue and we could always co-opt people as needed. Sometimes we only had four members at a meeting, but we did not feel disadvantaged.

More than ever now, we realized the importance of good communication and consultation. Fortunately, there were never any occasions when we couldn't use at least part of the church, but plans often had to be reorganized quickly.

I always ensured that the vicar was kept up to date, and she invariably came up with useful suggestions. I met with any individuals or groups who might be affected by my plans, and here I relied greatly on my team. They were involved in my preparations and were able to identify possible objections. They talked to their friends in the congregation, encouraged them to think positively, and at least be prepared to try something out even if they initially thought they wouldn't like it. Their readiness to meet a challenge was a great strength.

Keeping going

The team always needed a focus. The Profile was instrumental in giving us our first main focus and began the process of allowing the team to grow up. We learned to trust each other, to understand our differing opinions, and to speak our minds without fear of being criticized or ridiculed. We learned to work as individuals together, and we learned how to recruit people with expertise needed to fill a gap. Above all, the team gave me tremendous support through suggesting ways of approaching a task and methods of improving what I had done.

When I did my church placement in the second year they could not be so involved. To keep the impetus going we held two meetings with a more social than work-oriented focus. I had one assignment where the teenager of my team and her friends made me some superb visual aids for a sermon. Because during this period there was not much work for the team to do, we were able to get through some review and forward planning. Later, when much of my work became confidential, I didn't have quite as much to tell them about my progress. However, we were able to look at and then assess the sermons I had to preach and to have some initial thoughts on a service I was scheduled to lead at the end of that year.

A goal keeps a team together. The goal of supporting the OLM candidate is primary, but is often not enough on its own to give the support team sufficient purpose and identity. Sometimes my team felt superfluous and thought I was managing very well on my own. I needed to convince them from time to time that I really needed their ideas to incorporate into my work, their practical help and friendship and, of course, their prayers. I had to work hard to ensure that they felt valued, particularly after we lost yet another member to the demands of new employment and I wondered if I would have a team left by the third year. I tried shorter meetings of about half an hour held after morning worship just to keep in touch with them. I found I could then manage without the longer evening meetings when very few, often only two or three now, could attend. This greater flexibility of meeting times encouraged the team. They appreciated the importance of their role and were ready to find alternative ways of accommodating the work involved.

Relationships

It was important for me that the group could use its own initiative. The task might be prompted by my assignment, but they needed to feel that I could use some of their ideas in carrying out my task. For one assignment I had to prepare and conduct a service of prayer and meditation. My team, after discussion, decided they would like to explore 'negative feelings'. They came up with an outline service, suggested resources, materials and music, and then left me to put it all together. They perceived me as completely able and competent to provide a liturgy that met their needs. They were not ready to acknowledge that I might find the task difficult. I had never considered the issue of 'negative feelings' in any depth and was not at all sure that I could present it in a manner that would provoke thought and discussion in such a way that it would help them and the others who would attend the service. I produced the service and everyone who attended was generous in their appraisal. I am sure the team never really comprehended my doubts about my own ability to present a service of prayer and meditation on the topic.

Assessment

I always found assessment a problem, as it must be for anyone being assessed by those who work with them. I was an OLM candidate. I was on a course of study, and therefore I must be capable. Also, they had supported me in my application for this course. They had chosen to work with me. It followed that they did not want to find any weaknesses in me, and they concentrated on my strengths and assessed me accordingly. They did *so* much want me to do well. A more detailed critique would have been useful from them. They had the tools and criteria for assessment provided by the Scheme, and when pressed they came up with some very mild suggestions for improvement. But I could always rely on the vicar to be honest with me, and by the end of my course the team were much more open with me.

Review

My team and I worked through a great deal of trial and error and crisis. We were welded together in prayer, in our loyalty to our church – especially after the fire – and in our work together, which we could see would eventually benefit St Mary's. Looking back on the process, I think we placed too much emphasis on action and achievement and not enough on evaluating and using the evaluation in forward planning. We could have set ourselves some small, short-term goals, rather than the middle- to long-term targets that circumstances thrust upon us. Some targets are still not met five years on. We were constantly making do as we looked forward to new building and reorganization. But there were exciting moments when what we had prepared went well. As our confidence grew, we learned to experiment and take risks, we aired our doubt, and we listened to each other's opinions and continued to be optimistic even though we were going through a time of trial. We all learned leadership, Christian leadership, how to encourage others, how to answer questions of faith, and how to manage change. We developed better communication with other church members, some of whom took an active interest in what we were doing.

Beyond ordination

Half of the team still live in the parish, and we still support each other informally. They and others who became involved continue to serve the church using some of the interests they developed in supporting me. Those interests include the choir, the serving team, and liturgy. Three people have explored their own vocations and are moving forward on their own faith journey. The change over the last nine years has been considerable, partly because it was forced on us by the fire, but also because through learning to work together, forming groups to deal with a particular action and encouraging each other to seek and use our own skills and talents, we have developed in faith and understanding. God calls us to be what we are and I think we have learned something of what that means.

Facilitators

Candidates on the Ordained Local Ministry Scheme were, and still are, given excellent support, both academic and pastoral. Support given by parish groups varies considerably. In my year could be found teams that met regularly and worked hard all through the course, but there were also groups that did not operate as groups, though individuals gave their candidate good support. One group fell apart because so many of them moved from the parish. In 2001, team facilitators were recruited. They were drawn mainly from past students and given basic training in team management. Then they were appointed to go into each parish, initially to explain the function of the support team in relation to the candidate and the Scheme. The process of collaborative learning would be clarified and, if needed, the facilitator would help to train the group to work together. After two or three visits in the first term to ensure that the group understood their function in supporting the candidate, the facilitator would only visit again in May or June to review the team's progress during the previous year and to develop an action plan for the coming year. The facilitator's role is primarily to support the candidate, but the team could also call in the facilitator if problems arose. Following ordination I became a facilitator, and was appointed to support more than one team, as some others were.

My work with facilitators

Over the last two years I have been responsible for placing appropriate facilitators with support groups and for reviewing their work with them. As might be expected, diversity is the key finding. Candidates are individuals and diverse, and their groups are diverse too. Some facilitators are welcomed as extra help, as useful observers who give much-appreciated feedback. Others are initially distrusted, being seen as people who might interfere with the running of the parish. Several facilitators have found the groups were running so well that they were not really needed except for the annual review of the team's work with the candidate. In the course of our visits we have learned much about the way in which support groups can function and have identified some key elements in the composition of a supportive group.

Choosing companions for the journey

Choosing members of a support group takes time. It can be based on an existing ministry team, and this is likely to occur in a small church where I have seen such a group work well because they have worked closely together for some time and trust each other. Sometimes people expect to be chosen because of the position they hold in the church – for instance, as churchwarden or head server. This can lead to difficulties and can upset the working of the group if such people have exercised authority for some time and do not wish to see that authority challenged. They can be highly resistant to change. I have seen a team that found it very hard to discuss ideas for assignments and impossible to try a new approach to worship because of constant opposition to change. Then a particular person moved from the district and the difference was striking. Suddenly the atmosphere in the church changed, the candidate and team were more relaxed, and everyone was pleased to be able to put new ideas into practice without fear of opposition.

Firmness and tact both need to be applied in setting up a support group. I have been told of teams where the incumbent was chair and, as a result, the candidate did not have the experience of church leadership that is so valuable. The teams instinctively turned to the incumbent for guidance. In addition, the teams saw themselves as an extension of their church's ministry and, rather than being there for their candidate, they ended up putting the incumbent's plans for the church first. The candidate struggled alone, trying to fit coursework in with what had already been decided. One facilitator of a group like this managed to talk to the incumbent about the Ordained Local Ministry Scheme in detail, stressing the importance of being able to try out a liturgy with a group of people who would all contribute ideas. She persuaded the incumbent that his presence might well prevent any errors of judgement, but on the whole it would be better for the candidate to learn through his own, and the team's, possible mistakes. The incumbent's comments were welcomed *after* the service.

Facilitator as guide

We have found it important for the facilitator to meet with the team as early as possible so that the relationship can quickly be made clear. The incumbent sometimes feels threatened, as it can seem as if their role as leader is being diminished and their role in helping the candidate meddled with. The facilitator has to ensure that everyone understands that their role is to support the candidate and not to interfere with the running of the church. The team has to understand its function as a support for the candidate, to assess and review progress, and through example to enable growth in collaborative learning within the church. We have to take time to explain this and to build our own relationship with both candidate and team. We help them to create terms of reference (about, for instance, times of meetings, ways of reporting back to the PCC and congregation, and the organization of evaluation and assessment). Teams need time to bond. Often the tasks engendered by the production of the Neighbourhood Profile ensure this, but if bonding, trust and confidence are shaky then we use team-building exercises (see Belbin, 1981) or, through observing the teamwork, we note strengths and weaknesses and then give feedback on what we have seen with suggestions for change. The candidate has to be able to balance time needed for tasks with the time that can be allowed for team development and enabling the team to grow up.

Stages on the way

Change is always an important issue, and my background in education has given me much experience in the management of change. Some facilitators also have wide experience; others need guidance. Most teams do not appreciate that they themselves will change as individuals and as a team. As the candidate goes through the course, they develop as an ordinand, and as they grow, then so do those working with them. It is necessary for all to be kept up-to-date, and that means that there has to be clear communication and consultation. Again, the production of the Neighbourhood Profile proves the basis for good teamwork. The profile and any action plan derived from it needs to be publicized through discussion at PCC meetings and through presentations to the congregation. Everyone needs to be made aware where God is working in their parish, what resources there are, and where the church can either initiate action or just fill a gap. All this brings a team together as they use their talents and find others whose skills can contribute to the Profile and contribute to working out priorities for action. Members learn to trust one another, to appreciate their differences, to form and voice their opinions, to disagree with each other without getting upset, and to put the candidate's work first. I have seen teams really bonding and moving forward with enthusiasm and lively discussion. When it is my task to give feedback after a review and I have been able to say how much I have enjoyed a session which has illustrated how much they have achieved as a team and how well the candidate has progressed, the facilitator shares in the feeling of success.

But not all assignments provide as many opportunities for team-work as the Profile and teams need to adapt to times of relative quiet as well as times when there is much to do. Occasionally, when there is not much to do, a team can get diverted from support for the candidate. I have found it important that a team always has a goal to work towards.

Keeping the destination in view

The destination is ordination for the candidate and staying with the candidate to the end of the road. The composition of a support team might change and often has, but what matters is that the candidate has a core of reliable people who can work together and seize opportunities for sharing the work with others outside the team. To have a task in hand is essential for ensuring that members feel valued. The task can be small: for instance, decorating a pensioner's flat. Here there was a definite beginning and end and success could easily be measured. Work of this kind brings out the best in the participants. There is a common goal, the work is not too arduous, good humour and trust underwrite the action, and telling the rest of the team about it incorporates everyone in the task. This is a good example of collaboration concerned with learning and developing faith in the church community.

Other good examples of shared tasks include producing a parish magazine, starting a coffee morning, and making sure the church is known in the community it serves through advertising, sales of work, etc. Starting a prayer group was a task in one group and the prayer group's initiation and continuance became an important part of the church's mission. All of these tasks have been used by candidates in assignments, are in keeping with the aims of the Ordained Local Ministry Scheme, and have given me, as a facilitator, ideas for other groups as well as for my own church.

Lessons learned

The support team is essential for the well-being of the candidate. The size of the team and the continuity of all its members is not important. What matters is that there is always a group of people who are ready to be a good support and friend to the candidate.

Within the context of the Ordained Local Ministry Scheme, these people are planners, evaluators, reviewers, developers, knowledgeable about their church and district, and able to communicate with other groups and the congregation as a whole. They need to report to the PCC on the work they are sharing with the candidate. They need to be ready to assist in the preparation and presentation of worship and study sessions. By the time the course is completed I have found, both through my own experience and that of other candidates, that there are now people in the church who have developed skills in leadership and management, who have a picture of the place of their church in the community, and who have a clearer idea of what is needed and what they can contribute in the field of mission and evangelism.

The role of facilitator as a regular visitor, I feel, has become unnecessary when, as in most cases, the candidate has a strongly supportive team. A member of the Ordained Local Ministry Scheme needs to meet with the team at their formation, explain their function within the Scheme, and field questions. Teams need to know who they can call upon if necessary; but I have found that once they have started to work, have acknowledged and accepted their strengths and weaknesses, and have grown together, then they have generally gained the confidence to see for themselves the way forward. The essentials are time, and the ability to be adaptable, to have the courage to try something out, to learn from mistakes, and to be grounded in faith and supported by prayer.

Further reading

Belbin, R. Meredith, *Management Teams: Why They Succeed or Fail*, Heinemann, London, 1981.

Brown, Allen G., *Groupwork*, Wildwood House, Hampshire, 1989.

Handy, Charles, *Understanding Voluntary Organisations*, Penguin, Harmondsworth, 1990.

Nelson, John (ed.), *Management and Ministry – Appreciating Contemporary Issues*, Canterbury Press, Norwich, 1996.

8. The Incumbent's View

ALYSON PEBERDY

The Lord appointed seventy others and sent them on ahead of him in pairs to every town and place where he himself intended to go. He said to them, 'The harvest is plentiful, but the labourers are few; therefore ask the Lord of the harvest to send out labourers into his harvest'. (Luke 10.1–2)

My first impression of OLMs was that they come in pairs, like the 70 described by Luke. For in New Zealand they often do, and it was while worshipping one Sunday morning in a small rural church in the Bay of Islands that I first discovered the existence of OLMs. Two very recently ordained local deacons were being welcomed into their new role in the church that had sponsored them and had no vicar of its own. Over lunch in the church hall, various members of the congregation stressed the importance of the two working together to model and develop shared ministry, and not to be a vicar in the 'traditional' sense. This vision has been well described by Penny Jamieson, Bishop of Dunedin:

> Communities have called women (and men) from among their number to be priests, not in the sense of exercising leadership in a sole charge situation, but by working in a team with lay leadership, so that they are free to pursue the specifics of their priesthood, to gather the people of God around the holy table of God, without the burden of being on a pedestal. Their firm sense of location within and of the community of the baptised is a strong sign that priesthood is a gift that belongs to the whole people of God. So the challenge to the church is to move from a community that receives ministry to becoming a 'ministering community'.[1]

Unlike the 70 who were to keep moving, OLMs are meant to stay put, but their purpose is similar: to pray, to offer healing and peace, and to proclaim the nearness of the kingdom of God. In both contexts, the urgency of the task seems to leave little room or time to ask how this 'innovation' looks from the perspective of either the 12 or the stipendiary parish priest. Yet perhaps it would be wise to pause and raise this question, since simply having more workers does not *necessarily* mean that more work gets done. Productive collaborative ministry demands clarity, agreement and support, and it needs roles, responsibilities, patterns of authority and accountability to be agreed and evaluated. This is where questions about the incumbent's view and the relationship between Ordained Local Ministry and stipendiary parish priest become crucially important, especially in parishes where an OLM and a parish priest (with perhaps also a Non-Stipendiary Minister (NSM), a stipendiary curate, a Reader and a Southwark Pastoral Auxiliary) work side by side.

Those OLMs who are still working with the incumbent or priest-in-charge who initially supported their selection and training will tend to have developed a strong and possibly almost familial relationship with the incumbent who has acted as their patron. But what happens when the original incumbent has moved on and a new appointment is made? Without a supportive parish priest it is difficult for an OLM to flourish. The 1998 report on Ordained Local Ministry, *Stranger in the Wings,*[2] emphasizes the need for new incumbents to understand the nature and purpose of Ordained Local Ministry and to show evidence of a capacity to work collaboratively if they are to move to a parish with an OLM in post:

> . . . time and again . . .we have heard of instances where collaborative ministry has been fatally undermined by the making of an inappropriate appointment to the incumbency . . . the diocesan bishop should have unequivocal evidence of a prospective incumbent's commitment to shared ministry, and be sure it is not merely a commitment to delegation.[3]

It does not follow, however, that an incumbent with such un-equivocal evidence of a commitment to collaborative ministry will necessarily find the reality of working with an OLM easy. In 1999 I moved from a curacy in a well-staffed team ministry with a team rector, two team vicars, a Reader and an OLM in training to become vicar of a one-church parish in South London. I had never before lived or worked in London and enjoy being part of a team, so the presence of an OLM in my new parish was something I regarded as a definite asset. Here was a man, some 15 years older than myself, who had grown up a couple of streets away from the church and whose local knowledge and style of ministry would, I hoped, be likely to complement my own. I looked forward to having someone with whom to say the daily offices and generally share the joys and sorrows of priestly ministry, as had been the case in the team ministry from which I had moved. The OLM was not part of the interview panel, but we both recognized the need to meet and discuss the possibility of working together before a firm decision was made. On meeting, we felt we would be able to get on well together, though quite what our different assumptions were and what each of us was taking on we had yet to discover.

The experience of two previously unrelated priests, ordained at around the same time, trying to learn to work together in the same parish, is not straightforward, however much both parties want it to go well. All sorts of differences, perceived inequalities and role confusions come into play. I was full-time and paid, while my OLM colleague was two-thirds' time and completely unpaid. My experience of collaboration was in the questioning and fast-moving environment of the Open University, and then of a large team ministry, while his was as co-manager of a small family business. I was an outsider and arrived knowing no one; he had lived in the area most of his life, knew many members of the congregation from childhood, and expected to conduct their funerals. I was listed in the diocesan directory as the vicar and he as the honorary curate. I was female and officially 'in charge', he was male and not. The task of developing a mutually satisfactory pattern of shared ministry in this particular context occupied much of my prayer and practice during the first year and beyond.

Part of this chapter draws on my own experience and reflection, especially in relation to the complex, and often invisible, interplay of ecclesial authority and local influence which may either enhance or limit ministry and mission. Identifying this is important, but difficult in a wider Church in which the value and place of Ordained Local Ministry is often misunderstood, fundamentally questioned, and even denied. So I want to say very clearly that the purpose of this chapter is to help stipendiary and local ministers work better together. Like motherhood and apple pie, almost everyone says that co-operation and shared ministry are excellent things, but the questions are: How best are we to give them practical content at the parish, deanery and diocesan levels? And what gets in the way?

My own experience has been formative in my thinking about these questions, but it can be only one part of a much wider reflection. In order to capture something of the bigger picture, I have interviewed in detail 11 other incumbents or priests-in-charge from a variety of parishes and situations in this diocese, and have sought wider written comments. Of course, more would have been better, but so little has been written from this perspective that even a small number of interviews will yield new insights. Those who were interviewed were sometimes nervous of speaking publicly, as though they might be misusing their position, so care has been taken to alter potentially identifiable details. The first question I asked was about what parish priests hope for and value about working with an OLM.

What parish priests value most about working with an OLM

Most new incumbents usually view as enormously helpful the presence of an experienced colleague who knows the area and church well. Having someone to hand who can provide local infor-mation about people, places and organizations saves both time and effort:

> It's good to have someone in the parish who has been there for some time and knows it well . . . There were things we could discuss and reflect on together, pastoral issues, and where things had been going wrong. To have someone to reflect with in that kind of a way was very supportive.

In a large and busy parish the presence of such colleagues tends to be seen as essential rather than simply helpful. Stipendiary curates and Non-Stipendiary Ministers (NSMs) are also important here, but the OLM is a constant and stable presence who will not be moving elsewhere:

> For me, it was tremendously good that when I came as a total newcomer to my parish last year there were other priests there, both an OLM but also a curate in his last year. So I had two people who knew what switch did what. In a parish that was big and has a big workload, I don't think I would have been able to manage without someone like our OLM who knows the area and knows the church. It was just great having that kind of resource from the beginning and was definitely a plus and continues to be so. We need more than one person with experience in this parish.

Even in a small parish, the assistance of an OLM or NSM makes it much easier for an incumbent to take annual and study leave and go on retreat. I have complete confidence that my OLM colleague will look after things well in my absence. So for the incumbent, there are obvious advantages in having a well-established and reliable OLM.

But what are the advantages for the parish as a whole? In particular, does the existence of Ordained Local Ministry challenge the church to move from a community that receives ministry to becoming a ministering community? Several incumbents have commented on the contribution that Ordained Local Ministry training has made to the development of their parish. One spoke of the way in which the OLM ordinand is bringing a breadth of vision and contact with the wider Church that is missing from NSM colleagues who have been in that parish a very long time. Certainly, where a parish engages well with the selection and training of their OLM, the impact on that parish can be very stimulating, opening up new horizons and energy, sometimes more than the parish priest expects, and in surprising ways, as another incumbent describes:

> What we have enjoyed about having OLM students has been the way in which people in the congregation have enthused about the focus and approachability of the training. The way so many people have been part of their support group, and can understand what is going on has been marvellous. In fact, it has been quite difficult to actually hold the reins in on people who now say 'Look, we are doing all this stuff on mission for them, what are we going to do about it now for the sake of the parish?' I have to say, 'Let's get these people trained first'. That's what is exciting – it is a living example of people learning together and I've never seen that before.

In another parish, the priest valued the way congregational involvement in Ordained Local Ministry training has encouraged people to consider their own vocation too:

> It made a lot of people think about what is vocation. Our OLM in training was thinking about it for the clerical line, but paradoxically it made other people think about their lay vocation. It has put that question on the agenda permanently. Some schemes have not worked like that and have made people feel you only have a vocation if you are wearing a dog collar, but this one has not.

This incumbent, who was appointed after the OLM had been selected and was about to begin training, had no previous experience or understanding of Ordained Local Ministry. He describes himself as having doubts about 'the whole OLM thing' largely because of its purely local nature, but also spoke of valuing the fact that an OLM may choose to exercise a quite focused ministry – such as spiritual direction or pastoral care – rather than feel they should cover the whole range expected of a stipendiary or NSM:

> Some people may be hugely gifted in a particular area and the parish priest has to do everything, and whereas with a non-stipendiary we might feel irritated with the attitude 'Well, I'll do it if I want', I'm now feeling that's good because she can do what she is really good at. Never mind that she is not doing other things.

Other incumbents also speak of valuing the opportunity to develop the particular gifts of the individual rather than necessarily expect an OLM to be active and competent in all aspects of ministry. The OLM's perceived freedom to choose is something several parish priests almost envy, especially the freedom to avoid administration and responsibility for buildings. Yet specialist ministry is not the pattern followed by many OLMs.

Specialist or generalist ministry?

The most obvious influence on the scope of Ordained Local Ministry is the number of hours an OLM is available for the parish. This varies enormously: some are in full-time employment, while others are retired; some have dependants, others do not; some have very wide networks beyond the parish, while others are almost entirely parish-focused. At one end of the spectrum are those putting in as many hours a week as their parish priest, and at the other are OLMs who are hard pressed to be available to the parish more than a few hours a week. Within all this variation, the only common point seems to be the expectation that an OLM will be fully involved in leading worship most Sundays.

Although local ministry is often assumed to be almost entirely liturgical and pastoral, there is in fact no fixed pattern here. Some incumbents say that their OLM wishes to be involved in all aspects of ministry, including the more bureaucratic and administrative tasks. The reasons for this are mixed. Certainly some OLMs are very good at practical tasks and more experienced than the incumbent at looking after buildings. My own OLM had been churchwarden for many years and is generally better than I am at knowing what is wrong with the gutters or roof. The ordering of candles, completing of forms, and repair of the fabric was performed with great efficiency during the interregnum and some of these tasks he has simply held on to. I am relieved that he enjoys doing them, but as this is my first incumbency I do feel oddly deprived of the opportunity to understand what is required. Gaining this knowledge and experience has been very difficult, as parishioners tend to bring issues to do with the buildings to the person who best understands the problem.

It is not only male OLMs who want a completely generalist ministry that differs little from the incumbent's. The experience of another incumbent with an older, but female, OLM throws light on the way in which perceived differential status of the OLM and stipendiary may play a part in decisions about the scope of the ministry of an OLM:

> I thought I would find it easier if my OLM had a more specialist role. But she feels quite strongly because of the questions about status of OLM that she must be able to do all the things that the vicar can do . . . As we've got to know one another trust has developed and the working relationship is a good one . . . I have begun to see which kind of things she gravitates towards and I think she's beginning to let go of things she is not so keen on. So I think it will naturally develop that she will focus more on certain things.

Where an OLM has a wide-ranging ministry and a great deal of time to give to the parish, there is the possibility of role confusion and even competition with the parish priest. A clear and annually reviewed job description and working agreement is likely to help here, though some OLMs are very resistant to this, possibly seeing it as an unwelcome limitation. This means that arriving at a division of labour that makes sense to all concerned and is in the interests of the parish can be a slow and difficult process, calling for patience and what one incumbent describes as 'big-heartedness on both sides':

> It's important to reflect on your own work and areas of ministry and see what the OLM is doing to complement what you do and then let them get on with that.

Normally OLMs are expected to be very involved in the leading of Sunday worship, but there are different views about frequency that can become a source of discontent for both incumbent and

OLM. One point of view is that the OLM and incumbent will share equally the liturgical leadership, though incumbents can find this expectation difficult – especially when the OLM has little time for general parish life.

Where incumbents feel complete equality is inappropriate, they may either start as they mean to go on or gradually adjust the pattern they have inherited. Here are three examples of these different approaches. The first speaker is the priest who remains to be convinced by the Ordained Local Ministry concept:

> Having acquired two deacons in one year, I have been arranging the rota on the basis that I will always preside more over the community because it's my community, just as I chair the PCC – other people are doing it for me just as I do it for the bishop . . . In the working agreement with my OLM, we agreed she would only dress up three Sundays out of four, so she would have one Sunday a month to go to other churches or sit in the congregation.

The second speaker explains a similar decision in a more functional, less hierarchical, way:

> I'm of the opinion that if there are four Sundays, I preside twice and preach twice. The stipendiary curate and the OLM will each preside once . . . I wouldn't feel comfortable abdicating too much. The stipendiary curate will be gone in a couple of years and the OLM has little time for on-going pastoral care, so building the church up falls mainly to me. It's not about power and control, but about what I am seeking to build here and it's important that that doesn't fall apart when the stipendiary curate moves on.

The third describes making a gradual change to the pattern he found on arrival:

> What I inherited was everyone shares equally, which I'm sure must have developed during the vacancy. I don't think that would have been the style of my predecessor. So the first rota was actually done when I arrived. I thought I would just slot in and listen and see how it all worked, and then after a bit I might want to possibly change things. Now I do the rota and it became clear to me very quickly that I need to spend more time in the bigger church because I wasn't used to leading in such a big building with a large congregation and I needed to get the hang

of that. So the OLM is now more often down at our little church. And that's the pattern now.

In some cases, the process of adjustment is quite fraught – especially where there are several ministers wanting to be involved in the main service, but not available for the daily offices, early morning services, or routine tasks:

> Having a stipendiary curate and an OLM and a lay reader in training as well, and everyone wanting to participate on a Sunday morning, didn't leave much room for me. And there was a sense of wanting to take this position on a Sunday morning without any extra things during the week. No one else wanted to be doing the early communion. That felt very unfair. I had expected that OLMs and lay readers were there to augment my own ministry in the parish, but I feel sometimes it's now the other way round. I'm doing the little bits and pieces and everything, and other people are able to stand up there on Sunday morning having done very little else [in the parish] week after week. I suppose it's a matter of renegotiating the working agreement or making it clear in supervision and things like that. It catches up on you very quickly and you suddenly realize what's happened to you. Of course I am a servant, but putting the chairs away on my own . . . !

A recurrent theme for some incumbents is the difficult process of learning how best to work with an inherited OLM, and possibly other ministers too, when they have been far more active and influential during an interregnum than ever before. This raises some very interesting questions about both the local and wider Church's expectations of the OLM in an interregnum.

Minding the gap: what happens during an interregnum

The language we use automatically for the period between one parish priest leaving and the next arriving is a sharp reminder of the deeply embedded presence of a hierarchical model of the Church very different from that underlying the Ordained Local Ministry vision. Not surprisingly, OLMs faced with minding the gap find themselves under various pressures from themselves, their parish, and even sometimes their rural/area deans, archdeacons or bishops, to fill the gap by taking up the reins, without thought of where that will leave the next incumbent. Such a pattern is discouraged by the Ordained Local Ministry Scheme itself, which aims to select and train people capable of letting go when a new incumbent arrives, but the interviews show that without a firm and supervised model for an OLM during this period, almost anything can happen. One incumbent spoke of a running battle between the OLM, stipendiary curate and churchwardens about who was responsible liturgically. Another recalled the OLM saying that he had simply been asked by the area bishop to 'man the fort'. The OLM had so enjoyed doing this, that *after* the appointment he told the new vicar that parishioners were asking why he could not have been appointed himself.

Perhaps this example picks up and focuses on a wider confusion about the purpose of Ordained Local Ministry. Is it intended to complement and accompany stipendiary ministry and encourage lay initiatives, as most of the promotional literature indicates? Or, as financial constraints tighten, should we expect it to become a future norm, replacing some stipendiary posts by exercising local oversight as predicted in the first chapter of this book? Many laypeople and some OLMs fail to see why OLMs are not allowed to become parish priest when a vacancy occurs, regarding it as an arbitrary and unfair limitation. On the other hand, incumbents working with a partnership model and vision have serious concerns about the way the gap between incumbents is handled, proposing for instance an archdeacon-led initiative providing support and guidance for OLMs and churchwardens as soon as an interregnum is on the cards. In some parts of the Anglican Communion, there are specialist locum priests experienced in filling interregna. Perhaps such expertise could be used in the Continuing Ministerial Education (CME) programme for OLMs and area deans in this diocese.

Change and continuity

An earlier chapter has emphasized the extent to which OLMs can bring change and new energy to a parish. The interviews conducted for this present chapter paint a picture of incumbents generally very impressed by the style of training and the kind of exploration and questioning it encourages, especially in a parish that has seen little change in recent years. But the suggestion that OLMs are necessarily or predominantly agents of change in their parishes is not supported by the experience of some incumbents, as the following example illustrates:

During the first 12 months there were many pastoral problems I had to deal with that hadn't been sorted out. I was in constant conversation with my OLM about the way things are and the way things have been in the last ten years, and with him railing against where I'm going . . . The OLM can't see the problems that I see. There is a very negative way of people finding continuity and comfort in keeping things as they are and the OLM represents that desire to stay where we are for many people.

Sometimes such tensions surface at PCC and ministry team meetings with the OLM openly opposing a suggestion or proposal being made by the incumbent, whether it be the removal of some pews, new ways of raising money, or whatever. I recall my jaw visibly dropping when my OLM colleague took issue with a minor innovation I was proposing. Having been trained never to disagree with my incumbent in public, I had assumed this was a general rule. On reflection I can see that it is much harder to observe for someone who is permanently in the parish than for a transitory curate. But an OLM needs to be very aware of the extent of his or her influence. There is no doubt that an OLM can become a focus for some people's desire to hold on to what they know best, enshrining their hopes for comfort and continuity in a priest who will 'always' be with them. The danger is that if one priest is primarily identified with continuity and comfort and the other with challenge and change then such a split can easily be played on by parishioners in ways that may seriously limit personal, priestly and parish development.

Some recommendations

The recommendations made in *Stranger in the Wings*[4] provide a useful background that is worth revisiting and implementing (see Appendix 1). But some six years later, from the perspective of incumbents who have been working with OLMs, additional insights and recommendations are emerging that call for the following changes if the overall Ordained Local Ministry vision is to be effective here and now in South London.

Flexibility in responding to wider local needs

Several incumbents initiated discussion of this question. They pointed out that the definition of local as only one parish is very unhelpful when an incumbent is given more than one parish to care for or there are several vacancies in a deanery. This is very much a call for a more equal sharing of the load between parish priest and OLM, and not a blurring of the distinction between OLM and NSM. At the moment when an incumbent is asked to provide help in a neighbouring parish, it is the incumbent – not the OLM – who is required to go, but this is not always the right decision. Barely 18 months into my own post I was made priest-in-charge of two neighbouring and unrelated parishes in addition to my own. The only way to avoid very seriously damaging the developing relationship with my own parish was to ask my OLM colleague to do as much Sunday cover in the other parishes as I did.

Managing an interregnum

When an incumbent or priest-in-charge leaves a parish in which there is an OLM, it is important not to encourage or allow the OLM to change their style and scope of ministry in order to fill the gap. Area deans and archdeacons must make clear to the church-wardens, PCC and other parish ministers that the OLM is not acting priest-in-charge and that appropriate help will be given from the diocese. Without this kind of intervention and support, the subsequent relationship between the OLM and the new incumbent is likely to be far less productive and fruitful for the parish than it could otherwise be.

The possibility of transfer of category

As an OLM priest develops, there will need to be points of review at which it is possible to ask whether Ordained Local Ministry continues to be the appropriate category for this person. Occasionally, NSM or stipendiary ministry may be the right next step, and where this is being considered a diocesan transfer panel should be convened. There have already been some experiments in this direction, and consideration is being given to policy and regulations. A consistent policy and transparent process are essential.

A strange marriage

Ordained Local Ministry in Southwark Diocese has been changing from its inception and will doubtless continue to change. This means flexibility is vital, not only between OLMs and incumbents, but also at the level of diocesan and national policy. The stresses and strains encountered by the OLM and incumbent alike, and referred to in this chapter, are not marks of failure, but signs of the enormous effort required to combine two very different models of priestly ministry. This strange, and often arranged, marriage is bravely doing its best in a Church that tends to mask financial cuts with romantic rhetoric and is thoroughly muddled about what it is willing actively and honestly to support and reward. In the midst of this muddle, bishops, archdeacons, boards and councils must resist the urge, on the one hand, to stand back and let local clergy sort it out as best they can and, on the other, to react with *ad hoc* solutions or even a grand plan. A bit more flexibility, honesty and genuine consultation might simply be what are most needed, as indeed those of us who are trying to make this strange marriage work in the parish are already discovering.

Further reading

Jamieson, Penny, *Living at the Edge*, Mowbray, London, 1997.
Stranger in the Wings: A Report on Local Non-Stipendiary Ministry, Advisory Board of Ministry Policy Paper no. 8, Church House Publishing, London, 1998.
Southwark OLM Council, 'Ordained Local Ministry: Responding to Developments in Southwark Diocese', unpublished paper, 2004.

Notes

1 Jamieson, Penny, *Living at the Edge*, Mowbray, London, p. 49.
2 *Stranger in the Wings: A Report on Local Non-Stipendiary Ministry*, Advisory Board of Ministry Policy Paper no. 8, Church House Publishing, London, 1998.
3 *Stranger in the Wings*, p. 38.
4 *Stranger in the Wings*.

9. In Training

JEFFREY HESKINS

'Have you understood all this?' They answered 'Yes.' And he said to them, 'Therefore every scribe who has been trained for the kingdom of heaven is like the master of a household who brings out of his treasure what is new and what is old.' (Matthew 13.51–2)

I started training for ordained ministry 30 years ago. Having been to see Tony Tremlett, the then Bishop of Dover, as a young teenager, there was no question of how I would train. He wanted me to go to King's College, London, and he wrote to the Dean, Sidney Evans, and arranged an interview for me. Dean Evans was rightly proud of the set-up over which he presided. It was described as a unique course offering three years of academic life in a sizeable college of a university in a cosmopolitan city with all the resources and trappings a young student could desire. The three-year degree course was followed by a further year in community at St Augustine's College in the shadows of Canterbury Cathedral. It would be time spent in prayer, the discipline of the daily offices and Eucharist, and it would attend to the business of learning the craft of a priest. Preaching, teaching, leading worship and dispensing the sacraments, along with learning how to make a visit and take a funeral, were the details of its remit.

It might well have been a unique course for its time, but its components consisted of two central ingredients that throughout the history of theological training for priests and deacons in Western Europe have been held in perennial tension. Dean Evans lauded the experience of a thriving theological faculty taking its place in the world of other academic disciplines on the one hand, and the opportunity to withdraw in the context of an historic monastic setting on the other.

Training for Ordained Local Ministry is neither university training, nor seminary training, as it is neither principally academic theological learning set among other academic disciplines nor a residential community way of living and learning. Yet there are features to it that find their roots in the traditions of both, and there is a sense in which it is both seminary and academy, and neces- sarily so. In this chapter we will look at some of those facets of training encountered by candidates for Ordained Local Ministry and view them from the perspective of students currently under- going that training. Candidates involved in their final year of training have taken part in the collection of research data for this chapter. They have been invited to reflect on the comprehensive- ness of their training and on the effectiveness of its integration into the parish setting in which they have been called to serve. In the wider context of our received experience of training for ordained ministry, we might in this way discover whether locally focused training and the establishment of a new facet of understanding priestly ministry is something that is meeting the needs of the twenty-first-century Church. This will be pursued further in Chapter 10, which will listen to the experiences of OLMs currently serving in parishes.

It was Cardinal Pole who first used the word 'seminary' in connection with theological training.[1] The word meant a nursery garden, but it was introduced with a touch of irony, for in classical times it could denote a seed-bed of conspiracy. To what extent does contemporary theological training for OLMs remain a seed-bed, a place of nurture and growth? What are the ways in which they grow? Is there any sense in which their formation as seminarians, in a radical departure from traditional training programmes, is perceived as a conspiracy to produce a different kind of priest or different class of priest? Is there sufficient balance between the training gained from being in the world, and withdrawal from the world for reflection, meditation and prayer? In asking the students to reflect upon their experience of training in this way, we ask ourselves the core question that has dominated the history of theo- logical training: What is the most fitting context for the training of a priest?

Ordained Local Ministry: a post-modern ideology?

This question, however, needs to be preceded by a more funda- mental question that has never been properly asked in the training and formation of priests. What exactly are we looking to create? When I undertook my final year of seminary training, the Principal would remind us that in our provincial cathedral city the Theo- logical College stood at one end of town and the fish paste factory at the other; he would joke that in one sense it didn't matter what you put into either of them, it was what came out that counted. Sadly, it would appear that theological education with regard to training the clergy has, historically in Western Europe, had something of that feel to it. Issues like the perceived needs of the Church and the context in which the clergy are to serve have, until recently, not been a realized part of educational thinking.

Chief among the problems of seminary history since the Council of Trent have been issues of finance and control. How were colleges to be made economically viable and how much Episcopal influence was to be exercised within them? What these major problems of economics and power did was to sideline the question as to what kind of priest was required. The history of the seminary sees the answer to this question fluctuate between two distinct ideologies. The first was to create a safe place set apart from the world where the ordinands could have something of an extended retreat while learning the basics that would enable them to administer the sacraments, understand something about canon law, and preach without making complete fools of themselves. The second was almost the opposite. During the Enlightenment period the move to prevent seminarians reading Rousseau or Voltaire patently failed, as did the attempt to prevent the students wearing wigs rather than having tonsures.[2] Priests were clearly to live and minister within the world and were thus perceived to understand some of the ways of the world: how it works and thinks.

These two broad ideologies have jockeyed for pole position since then and it is perhaps only in the development of Anglican regional training schemes generally, and the Ordained Local Ministry Scheme in particular, that they have in any way managed to properly meet in an attempt to coexist. One final characteristic to emerge from seminary history has, wittingly or unwittingly, influenced the formation of Ordained Local Ministry. In its obsession to make training financially viable, the post-Enlightenment Church embarked on a drive to close local seminaries and instead opt for nationally controlled institutions.[3] These were resented and fiercely resisted. A local training somehow meant that local people knew what kind of local priest they might see emerge.

A local training partnership

There is a sense in which that is where the Ordained Local Ministry Scheme begins. Those training on the Scheme find themselves in a direct relationship of accountability to, and partnership with, the

community they have been called to serve. It is a theological training that finds itself rooted in a very particular context. Furthermore, this context enables a radical review of what theological
education might be. Other models of training often seem to present
a direct relationship between the student and the teacher, in which
it could be said that the one imparts knowledge to the other. By
way of contrast, the form of training adopted for Ordained Local
Ministry has to adopt a self-consciously different model which
involves a degree of sharing with the congregations that are to be
served. The result is that a different educational dynamic emerges:

> . . . you are never allowed to get away with being just academic.
> Everything is designed to have a practical application and every-
> thing is related to your context. The course has enabled me to
> grow on all levels. I love the connection with the parish and I like
> the fact that I am taught by people who see this as a learning
> experience for them as well. It never comes across as though they
> are the experts who have got something to teach and we just
> soak it all up.

This is pivotal to Ordained Local Ministry training and is clearly
something that is enjoyed by the ordination students participating
in it. Learning happens in a different way. Rather than seeing it as
something that merely provides a particular standard of education
or a level of skill that enables them to perform a task, this form of
learning is essentially a reflective one in which the student shares
with members of the congregation they are to serve not only
what they have learned, but how they have learned it. It is thus a
means by which the student becomes an independent learner with
unlimited scope as to what they might go on to discover.

The Ordained Local Ministry Scheme not only requires a partnership of discernment between candidate and congregation (as
already outlined in an earlier chapter) as to the calling to priesthood: it also requires those same people to take responsibility for
the formation of priesthood. One of the first things that an
Ordained Local Ministry student is required to do is to establish
adequate systems of support. For some, this is a group that already
exists within the church community they come from:

> My husband is extremely supportive and I think that the congre-
> gation understand what is going on, but I haven't created a huge
> support team or anything like that. There is a staff team that I
> belong to and we meet once a week and I do feel that I can tell
> them things and ask them to pray for me and the like.

Others have identified particular people that they have wanted to co-operate with for the duration of the training period and to whom they give account. It clearly needs to be a group within which the student can feel loyalty and trust:

> The support group that we had to create has worked very well and they really are supportive. It is made up of people that I have known for a long time and the vicar and I discussed the membership of the group.
>
> I think that I have been very lucky. I have had sound support, which I think has emerged from an understanding of what OLM was all about from the very beginning. It was as though the support emerged from a naïve understanding of the concept and then stumbled into a clear understanding. They are genuinely interested people on this support team who rightly see it as a faith development thing for themselves and that has been very affirming and encouraging for me, sharing that experience at that level.

So support is integral to the training, and through it is derived a sense of corporate discovery and learning. Even if there is only basic understanding of what the course is about, an early commitment to working together is seen as a commitment to learning together. This is an essential feature of the training dynamic and needs to be in place if the ordination student is to feel secure within the process. Unlike residential training, there is no established pattern imposed to regulate the training in the sense that there is no round of daily prayer done corporately as a learning body, no daily meals taken together, or day-to-day time spent with each other. But other patterns appear instead. The students meet one evening a week and are committed to four residential weekends together each year. They belong to peer groups, and each candidate has personal tutorials. Four study days a year are set aside for learning together while everything else is worked out in the parish through the support and learning systems that they have established for themselves. These systems are to a degree self-regulating, which means that they require a maturity of personnel. It is a very adult way of learning from the moment of its conception.

How much of this is appreciated by the wider congregation is difficult to gauge. The students perceived clearly that the core group they had established, or the staff team they belonged to, or the PCC they accounted to, had a fairly good idea as to what the training was about and what their responsibilities to it were. However, they were also clear that most of the congregation had only a basic understanding of what was happening. The larger a congregation, the more likely this was to be the case:

> Most of the congregation are not really interested in what I am doing and I am not saying that in a bad way. It is a large congregation, and so by way of things with large groups there are a number who simply don't know or are interested in other things that are going on. There is a nucleus of people who do, but they tend to be involved with a lot of things in the church anyway. It is interesting, many didn't know what OLM meant and I spent a lot of time explaining it.

Most congregational members seem simply to be glad that someone they know and like from their community is going to be ordained and is not going to leave them. This was particularly true of parish communities with the experience of ordination students called to stipendiary or non-stipendiary ministries:

> On the whole, those others who generally ask me how I am getting along in a polite sort of way do understand the concept. They have had the experience of other ordinands in the parish train and then go away and they know this is not going to happen with me. But then there are also a number of others who clearly don't understand the concept and I don't think that is a problem at all. I think that when my ministry affects them, then that will be the time for them to understand a bit more about it. A sort of realization by experience.

By nature, the course is very task-oriented, but most of the congregations seemed to respond to their part in the tasks out of loyalty to the student rather than out of curiosity for the task or the course. Some students expressed genuine surprise at these levels of support from the wider congregation:

> The first time I preached at an evening service a lot more people came than would usually turn out at that time and they did it to support me. So too, a few weeks ago I did my special service which the course makes us prepare with others for the congregation and there were many more than normal.

While all found high degrees of support within the congregation and various levels of understanding, one student noted that some in the congregation had wondered what effect the training might have upon the person they were supporting. If they were having a

share in making the priest, was the cost to be that of losing the
friend and the person they had related to differently all those
years?

> I think I have detected some suspicion about whether this
> change into a member of the clergy will actually be changing me
> as a person. I am a bit concerned about that, but hope they are
> things that will work themselves out.

This is a moot point. My own recollection of students in residential
training was, in a few instances, to witness some individuals
undergo the strangest metamorphosis during their training and
emerge as caricatures of clergy rather than compassionate human
beings. While I would not want to declare this to be any more than
the exception to the rule, it does seem more likely that the risk of
cultivating a caricature of the self is seriously diminished in a con-
textual setting for training where the community can more readily
challenge the symptoms. Conversely, the local church community
might also want to challenge something they see emerging in the
ordination candidate that might be deemed a feature or development that no longer fits the local church's ethos. While Ordained
Local Ministry training relates all learning to the local context, the
candidates are also drawn from different contexts and learn alongside each other. They are thus exposed to the influence of different
traditions, different understandings of what it means to be Church,
and different interpretations of those things through their learning
peers. The candidate sent for training might well return having
learned and experienced things that their local church are not
supportive or approving of. How they face or absorb any changes
they see in their ordination candidate will often challenge the
commitment to learning together. Occasionally it has led to
complete withdrawal of support for the candidate which, as will be
seen in the next part of this chapter, has serious theological implications for the whole integrity of Ordained Local Ministry as a
calling and raises concerns about the pastoral care of the candidate
and his or her colleagues. Much hinges on the local church leadership in such instances.

The role of the incumbent

The role of the incumbent in Ordained Local Ministry training is
much more clearly defined than in any other form of ordination
training, and this issue has already been explored in Chapter 8.

In residential and regional training, once a candidate has been selected for training, the parish incumbent has little official responsibility. They act as a support in a training system that they understand, since it is one that they are likely to have undergone themselves, but accountability is between the student, the course director and the bishop who has sponsored the training. The sending incumbent is only ever thereafter involved in an official capacity if the candidate does not complete his or her training. In Ordained Local Ministry training, the relationship between the incumbent, the course directors and the candidate for ordination is more developed. This really necessitates a high level of conversion, commitment and understanding from the incumbent. In other words, the incumbent needs a vision of what Ordained Local Ministry might mean in the parish, beyond simply having an extra pair of hands to ease a busy workload. Some students found that their incumbent had such a view:

> I think my incumbent understands the concept of what it means to be a Locally Ordained Minister very well. When we have met on a one-to-one basis he has been able to help me a lot particularly when things have been exercising me. He also thinks that it is a very good way of training, and sees clearly the differences between this way and the way that he was trained. I think that means that he has a lot of respect for the course.

> As I was thinking about what form of training I would take for ordination, it was my incumbent who encouraged the OLM route, and her arguments were persuasive because she knew the differences between the styles of training that were available. She could see that this training was better suited to me and my situation. She is a supporter of the theology behind the course and sees it as an innovative way of developing church leadership. I think that we are all going to benefit from that.

In these two instances, the conversion of the incumbent to the concept of Ordained Local Ministry has clearly been made. The effect of this is not only to lend the appearance of support, but to generate a feeling of security in the student and inspire confidence in the working out of the course in practice. There is little doubt that the downward side of this method of training for ministry is that it is reliant on the continuation of a positive attitude at grass-roots level and on the goodwill of the incumbent. There have been instances where, either through a change of heart by the incumbent and the local church, or through an inability to deal with how the ordination student changes as a result of training which then challenges the traditions or received ethos of the local church, support has been withdrawn. These have proved damaging experiences. If the call to be locally ordained is later deemed to be not a call at all, or a mistaken call, or a call that the incumbent and local church don't like any more, there is little that the candidate can do. His or her position is thus quite vulnerable, as some noted in relation to an instance where one of their student colleagues was indeed withdrawn from training:

> We had the experience of one of our members leaving the course because his church withdrew support for him. I did know that he was having difficulties about this because he shared this. So I wasn't surprised, but I was rather angry that his church hadn't thought through this in advance.

An experience like this has the effect of disturbing and distracting the entire year group in training, for they had grown in affection for one another as the course had progressed. There is grief to manage in the loss of a student colleague, and perhaps the realization that nobody on the training programme can assume that by entering the training they will automatically finish it. But the upward side to a training programme set out in this way is its very personal nature, and a significant bonding between the members of the group. This is because the current experience of OLMs in training is that they exist in relatively small numbers. In terms of running such a course, while there might be questions of financial viability, there is clearly more opportunity for personal attention in the tutor–student relationship and a chance for deeper bonding between the students themselves, which certainly serves them well in times of crisis or when they feel under pressure. This was evident among the sampled group when they lost their colleague. Their vulnerability as a group revealed, in the first instance, an illogical but understandable frustration and anger with those deemed to be able to do something about the situation:

> The group got rather angry with the course director because we felt his parish had let him down and so the course ought to be supporting him and I guess we all hoped that he would be able to find another parish and stay on the course.

It then moved to a rational and realistic understanding of the nature of what it means to be called locally to serve locally.

Now with hindsight we can see it is all rather more complex and there seem to have been political issues further up the line. You just can't march into another parish and demand that they take you on. It is unrealistic.

For some, it raised anxieties about their standing within their own communities. Could the same fate befall them?

Then we heard he had had to withdraw from the course. It made us all very angry because it was as though he had become a political pawn and it made some of us feel quite vulnerable too.

For others, their powerlessness – beyond letters of support to their colleagues – grew into a general resignation that this was a matter that affected them, but was beyond their grief:

We all wanted to stay in touch, but then as a group we reached a stage of realizing that it was probably kinder to leave it because he needed to face the fact that if he were to resume the course, it wouldn't be with us and he would need to move on in himself.

For the remaining students, the pastoral care seems to have been plentiful, as were the ensuing questions about how such a situation came to exist in the first place:

Ours has been a close group, and this matter upset us quite a bit because we didn't understand what was going on. It all seemed to be politics and it all should have been sorted out beforehand. The course tutors were really good and spent time with us when we got upset and annoyed. That took the pressure off us, though there was nothing we could do for our colleague. That was the mainstay of the course. There were plenty of people around for the few of us.

The whole issue of collaboration is strongly emphasized in OLM training, and it throws up a lot of questions about whether the course, its running, its constituents and the such like were properly explained. Did his congregation understand?

I think they didn't realize what they were letting themselves in for. I get a feeling that incumbents at the start don't really grasp what the OLM course is all about prior to selection. I think that a lot of them get quite a shock when they see what style of training it is.

It may well be that some incumbents are shocked at what they find, but there seemed to be some evidence of instances where, despite having a tenuous grasp of what the training is about, one or two manage to revel in the discovery:

> I think at first that he didn't know what it was and thought it to be rather similar to NSM training. However, since I have gone on with the training, he thinks it is a fantastic way of training and he wishes that he had been trained in some of the ways that he sees happening for me. I think that I would like more advice and support from him, but on the other hand I have to do this myself. Some of my colleagues have incumbents who are on top of them all of the time, telling them what to do, and so I feel that I am quite fortunate. He knows what is going on, but leaves me to my own resources unless I call for help.

There are still other incumbents who find that (much as some parents find the demands of their children's extra-curricular school activities) the course is very demanding of time and attention, requiring alterations to regular patterns of parish life and liturgical patterns throughout the year:

> I know that my incumbent feels it is a bit intrusive at times and has said so to the course administrators. It is as though it is taking things over, with deadlines being set by the university which might not fit in with the parish year just because a particular assignment has to be in on time.

Commitment and understanding clearly require a high degree of patience and a preparedness to communicate well with the training course staff. This is now particularly important since the Scheme has been validated at university level. The merits of this evolution incorporating the academy will be looked at later in this chapter by students, and in the next chapter by those who have lived through the changes from a seemingly straightforward, practically based training programme to one that has more academic stature. For the present, it needs only to be noted that the incorporation of university accreditation brings a third partner into play in the dynamics of the training relationship. Any relationship dynamic that accumulates partners will constantly have to review the ways in which the partners communicate.

Ordained Local Ministry: reflective training

As I have already outlined, the history of seminary training in Western Europe saw a swing in emphasis that reflected perceptions of quite different needs for the clergy in different ages. On the one hand, the 'seed-bed' vision of Cardinal Pole led to a residential training that was like a long retreat with plenty of opportunity to pray and think, withdrawn from the world and its influences. On the other hand, the influence of the Enlightenment period challenged this perception and instead provided for an academically rigorous training in the company of the newly emerging scientific disciplines of the period. What kind of training is Ordained Local Ministry training?

Clearly, it is a practical training in that much of what is required of the ordination student is task-oriented. Their assignments are focused on situations that they will find in the parishes to which they will return to serve as priests. It is also clear that participants have now to buy into a level of academic acumen that was not there at the inception of the vision and programme that became the Ordained Local Ministry Scheme. In that sense, the course has adopted some of the features of its historic seminary inheritance. However, this is a course to train clergy, and we should ask what time and space is accorded to prayer, worship and reflective practice? For some students, the course programme is something that seems rather stark in this area. In one sense, this is understandable. With the number of occasions on which the students meet and spend time together so restricted, it is fairly near impossible to establish a corporate pattern of prayer and reflection:

> I am not sure that the training is reflective enough. I find the pace rather fast at times. Besides, the problem is not whether we have enough prayer time or not, but that there hasn't been any space for something like an away-day for a quiet time or a retreat.

For others, this is not seen to be the principal purpose of the training. If it is indeed a training programme that points the way rather than takes them through everything, then while they certainly find few opportunities to develop a spiritual and prayer life as a corpus, they learn the importance of it and how to go about setting it up for themselves:

> Each time we meet we always start with an act of worship led by each of the course members in turn. The weekends that we are away have a number of opportunities where we can have a

spiritual focus and each of the weekends has a different slant to it. So I have discovered things like Ignatian spirituality and done things like praying with icons and that sort of thing. The course is presented in such a way that you go away wanting to learn more about it.

Herein lies an important insight as to the type of candidate called for Ordained Local Ministry. So much of this course is driven by the requirement to be able to learn about learning in order that the candidate can go and find out things in their own time, that it demands a developed personal maturity and inner resourceful-ness. For some candidates, this has opened them up to challenges of faith that they have gladly met head on:

> I think that the course in its entirety is spiritually driven and I think that it has helped me see that no matter where we think we are on the Christian pilgrimage we cannot assume that we have already arrived. The type of teaching we have is one that encour-ages us to ask questions of ourselves, getting us to look at things a little closer for greater understanding. It peels away assumed positions of faith. In my case I have discovered that there is always room for growth and a movement further and deeper into faith.

For others, this encounter has been rather daunting, and not always an easy place to be in:

> When I read the Bible, I like to look at it from different angles and reflect through the Holy Spirit, if you see what I mean. I have found aspects of the course very mind and brain centred at times with a lot of questioning, and turning round some of the things that seem to me to be God's Word and which are all part of the tradition that I inhabit.

For still others, it has both emphasized the need to be an inde-pendent learner and a reflective practitioner in order to take on the rigours of ordained ministry. Reflective practice is something of a buzz phrase in the world of practical theology and ministerial training – something reckoned to be good and appearing on the syllabus of most training courses. However, when the surface is scratched it could quite easily be regarded as tokenistic. There is even less evidence of clergy in training parishes making use of it with their newly ordained assistants, or of it featuring in any kind of post-ordination or continued ministerial training programmes.[4] The Ordained Local Ministry training course would seem to go some way to challenging that tokenism, but even here, some observed that there were shortcomings:

> I think that in all the work we do we are required to reflect about what we are learning and how it relates to our context. Some of the pastoral assignments and placements have required us to reflect more upon the impact of the experience on ourselves. However, it could be built into others too as I don't think it is there in all of them. I have never heard anyone teaching the course particularly sell the idea of spiritual direction. It might be that they look at this with individuals, but it doesn't seem to be a general thing. I feel that if you are already quite a reflective person, that is a good thing and is supported, but I am not sure that it is challenged if you are not.

Ordained Local Ministry: a changing training experience

In its genesis, the Ordained Local Ministry Scheme was clearly intended to be a radically different kind of training programme offering a course that was unashamedly centred on a commitment to praxis. Part of the attraction of the scheme was that it did not involve the academic demands found in university courses, seminary training or regional schemes. The risk of such a training programme was that it could have encouraged the adoption of an elitist attitude among the clergy, with a lower regard for a priest trained on a practice-centred scheme. What has happened to Ordained Local Ministry training as it has evolved is that it has become subject to, or victim of (depending upon your perspective), the reforms in theological training nationally. A vision for theological education beginning and driven from the grassroots of the Church and centred on the local church is now monitored and accredited by the world of the academy. So, how true to its original vision has the present training programme been able to remain, and how far has it had to stray? Or does it remain a radical training vehicle while undergoing reform?

It is clear that the commitment to praxis that the Ordained Local Ministry Scheme was originally defined by remains the most attractive aspect of the course. Students across the spectrum, regardless of their age, ethnicity, gender, church tradition, class background or educational experience, were unanimous in their declaration of this. This commitment as the core of the Scheme's ethos brought them an endless supply of opportunities for learning that they might otherwise never have gained or appreciated:

I think the placements were excellent. You get opportunities you would never get otherwise to become immersed in something and really become involved and part of it, which is really quite different from going on a day visit somewhere. So, practically, it is very good.

The more I learn, the more I want to know. What I do feel is that I am gaining in confidence to tackle the things that are challenging me. It is good to be aware of what you don't know. Our Doctrine teacher is really making us all think and it is challenging us to define our own feelings and beliefs so that we are clearer in our minds what we believe and how we communicate that to others. We are doing this through the experience of group exercises and discussions, and it is really helpful.

I think that the modules on counselling and bereavement were very helpful and practical, and I think that there must be more emphasis on that aspect throughout the training. It is so important for ministers and leaders to learn how to listen and not do all the talking.

This emphasis upon a learning system that takes experience seriously is clearly a feature that attracts a good proportion of students to the course in the first place. As a general rule (though not exclusively), the candidates attracted to participate in the course tend to be mature students. The youngest selected for training in the sample surveyed for this chapter was in her mid-forties. This is unusual, as will be seen in Chapter 10, where all those taking part in the research were in their senior years as citizens of pensionable age. The type of person likely to be attracted to priesthood as an OLM is someone who has inhabited the world of work for many years and, if they undertook any training for a profession, will have done so quite some time ago. For many such people, and for those who never undertook academic training at all, the prospect of a self-consciously academic course is not a particularly attractive one. For some, the increased emphasis on academic excellence has been testing at the most fundamental levels:

When I started out I was given the impression that it was not as academic as some of the other courses. But because the course is now authenticated as a degree course, I think that now there is quite a large element of the academic attached to it. When I started off I didn't even know how to turn a computer on. Yet everything has to be handed in formally, presented via the computer with bibliographies and so on. It had been a long time since I had done any of that kind of training, and so it was particularly difficult at the beginning.

It is important to pay attention to comments like these when candidates are considered for training as there is a general assumption that computer literacy in a hi-tech age is the norm when it is clear that for senior candidates familiarity with word processing and electronic mail should not be assumed.

Having said that, no candidate felt that the training course as it stood was overly academic and most felt that the course directors were establishing the right kind of balance between the traditionally academic, and the commitment to experiential learning accompanied by a period of in-depth reflection. The difficulty with presenting a course of this kind, now with a distinct academic bias, was – for some – how to deal with the challenges parts of it can present to the faith you have been nurtured in when there is so little time with the members of the course staff themselves:

> There is one area that worries me. When I did my degree in theology what happened for me was that my relationship with the Bible was deconstructed, which can be a disturbing experience, but then there was time to rebuild in a different way which was rather more academic. I am not convinced that in what we do there is the space or time necessary to do that. I think that for some people the unsettling stuff happens and I am not sure there is the time to do the re-constructing stuff, and I think that for some people that can make them quite defensive.

This is a useful insight and is perhaps another good argument for ensuring that the right kinds of support systems, in the form of spiritual direction and the like, are in place for the candidate preparing for ordination in this way.

On the relative merits of the shift in emphasis towards a more academically centred training for OLM candidates, the jury is still out. It is clear that for some the change has been an unwelcome struggle and unwarranted in terms of the way they perceive Ordained Local Ministry fitting into the general jigsaw of what it means to be a priest working in a parish system:

> I don't think that I would cope if it was more academic and I think that we always have to remember what we are being trained for. We are not going to be parish priests in the sense that we are going to be the principal leaders of a church. I know that you have got to have some theology and you have got to be able to preach properly, but you are not going to be the academic brain of the parish – I don't think. I see the role as being involved with pastoral care and linking with the community.

For others, it is a necessary development and one that they welcome for as long as it remains intelligently accessible and not
remote – and thus divisive when trying to incorporate it into life as
a parish priest with church members and parishioners:

> It is very practical, but I think that the course has moved much
> more towards being academic which I think is a good thing. For
> me this has been excellent because it has been very accessible
> and has reminded me of what was already in my bones, but
> which you sometimes forget is there.
>
> What I think is good is that it seems as though the course
> director acts as a kind of buffer between the university and us to
> get the balance right.

For still others, the concentration on learning for life has been the
liberating factor and the most appreciated feature of training. What
this warrants is the kind of 'positive protection' from the course
staff that the student describes here as part of the overall strategy
to build confidence, and a positive commitment to enabling the
candidates to know how learning happens and how they can best
use that within the course and beyond:

> We are being taught theology but perhaps more important we
> are discovering where to look for it. It is important to move
> beyond the introduction of whatever it is that we might be
> studying and try to dig for ourselves. There is a lot there and it
> relies on the students responding in this way. I think there is an
> intelligent mixture of theology and practice, and I think that one
> of the reasons why the OLM course works so well for me is that
> it has similar sympathies to the church context I come from. Both
> are open to difference and learning from difference, and com-
> mitted to an uncharted journey into life and ministry.

Is this an adequate training for ordained ministry? Certainly the
criticisms of it as preparation for ordination were few. Its shortcomings were plain to see, but everyone in the research sample
seemed well aware that no training of itself would completely
equip them for what awaited them. We now turn to how all of this
works itself out in the day-to-day practicalities of parish life for the
OLM.

Notes

1 Pole summoned a synod of the Church of England in November 1555. Its decrees first used the term 'seminary', which were later adopted at the Council of Trent in 1563.

2 Chadwick, Owen, 'The Seminary', in Sheils, W. J. and Wood, Diana (eds), *The Ministry: Clerical and Lay*, Blackwell, Oxford, 1989, p. 16.

3 Chadwick, 'The Seminary', p. 21.

4 See Heskins, Jeffrey, 'Essentially Reflective', in Torry, Malcolm (ed.), *The Parish: People, Place and Ministry: A Theological and Practical Exploration*, Canterbury Press, Norwich, 2004, pp. 187–8.

10. Being Ordained Local Ministers

JEFFREY HESKINS

Jesus sent him away, saying, 'Return to your home and declare how much God has done for you.' So he went away, proclaiming throughout the city how much Jesus had done for him. (Luke 8.39)

Ordained Local Ministry: the face of local continuity

When Simon Aleyn was made Vicar of Bray in 1540, he can hardly have expected to have presided continuously over the same parish during a period of political change that saw Henry VIII, Edward VI, Mary and then Elizabeth all take the throne of England. In that time he was first a Catholic, then a Protestant, then a Catholic again, and then once more a Protestant. Thomas Fuller wrote of him that he had seen some martyrs burnt (2 miles off) at Windsor, and found this fire too hot for his tender temper; and when accused of being a turncoat, Aleyn famously replied: 'Not so, for I always kept my principle, which is this, to live and die the Vicar of Bray.'[1]

This is what he did. For nearly 50 years he remained in post as the parish priest, irrespective of the changes that went on around him, committed to the life of the community in which he had come to find himself and the care of the souls in his charge.

In terms of his length of stay, Aleyn's life as a parish priest is not such an unusual one. Even until 20 years ago it was possible to find clergy whose tenure had extended 20 or 30 years or more. I now know of only two priests local to me whose continued stay in the same parish has exceeded 25 years. They are each well-known and much-loved local figures, and both were recently nominated for an MBE by local people in recognition of services to the local community.

The Church in Western Europe has witnessed an unprecedented amount of change in society within the last century. Much of that change has found its way into the Church as well. Some of it has clearly been for the good, but there is still an underlying tendency for many (often on the edge of the Church) to look to the Church as a place of consistency and continuity. It belongs to a mentality in which the familiar is somehow comforting and to be relied upon. It is always there.

A quick glance through *Crockford's Clerical Directory*,[2] however, will tell you that, with a few notable exceptions, Anglican stipendiary clergy, like clergy of most reformed traditions, move around with a degree of frequency. Change is considered to be good. Livings are often suspended pending 'pastoral reorganization', which usually means that those administering the parishes of the diocese are looking to manage on fewer resources – in other words, fewer paid clergy. Church communities are being asked to do more with less and to learn different ways of coexisting with one another. All of this has been a feature of life, in particular since the 1960s.

However, the greatest need often calls out the greatest resourcefulness in terms of creative human thinking, and with the loss of continuity and stability as the Church's ordained representatives choose and often need to move with greater frequency than their forebears, it might be argued that the advent of the OLM is one of the means with which these particular needs are met.

Whatever else they might be seen to be, OLMs can represent the face of continuity, and to some extent consistency, in the face of what is perceived as unrelenting change. That is not to say that they are to be seen as a resistance to change, for they themselves represent a change in perception of what it is to be a priest in a parish, and the fact that they represent this change might mean that they are a critical ingredient within the church local in a Church national that has undergone momentous change in the last 50 years. This chapter will attempt to reflect with a sample of OLMs on what it is like to minister with a particular local brief to a particular context and setting.

The clergy sampled for the research in this chapter were a mixture of difference: some women, some men, and of different ethnicities. Each served a different category of community, of which some were urban, some rural, and some from the suburbs of London. Most had been ordained priest for three or four years, and one was still in deacon's orders. All were well established in the communities they had been called to serve and most had undertaken a variety of different ministries in the local church.

I have been in the parish for the whole of my life from the time I was baptized at the church more than 70 years ago.

I have been in the parish for 62 years since the day I was born. I went with my parents as a child.

I have been here all my life. I started in primary Sunday school and have been here ever since. So my time here has gone over 60 years. From the Sunday school I eventually moved into the uniformed youth work and eventually became a leader in that work. I taught in Sunday school, joined the PCC, and was even a churchwarden. So I did quite a bit before I looked at ordination. Of the 60 years in the parish, I have spent my last four as an OLM priest.

Even the least 'established' in the community they had come to serve as a priest, had been part of that community for 14 years (although I am aware that there are others who are called with significantly less time in a parish, and that the minimum requirement for a calling to Ordained Local Ministry is three years). In terms of establishing a high degree of confidence and trust with the congregation, this lengthy period of settlement in a local community is a key feature in discerning a vocation and enabling a congregation to take responsibility for supporting the call to ordination. Two people had also found that their work brought them into contact with the wider local community – something they found of invaluable significance in considering this type of ordained ministry:

I have been involved as a church pastoral community worker in a family centre where I got to know a good many of the people who live in our local community.

I was a teacher at our local church school for well over 20 years. I had to help plan worship and productions which brought me into contact with the church as well as the parents with children at the school.

So the commitment to remaining a local figure and gaining the confidence of those in the local community for whom it will make a difference is all critical. Because those to be ordained as OLM have this particular localizing factor that is unique to their calling, not only is it helpful to have this commitment, but there needs to be a particular love for the parish they are going to serve. One person, in trying to discern her vocation, found a chance encounter with an OLM who offered this insight to be a deciding factor in agreeing to go forward for ordination.

I didn't think that I did want to become an OLM. I thought I might be cut out to be a pastoral auxiliary – which is something that would appeal to my strengths as a pastoral kind of person – and I thought the whole thing would just go away. But it didn't, and it just went on nagging at me. Then I met an OLM from a church near to mine and he said that OLMs need to love their parish, and the more he spoke the more I could see myself in everything he said. Then I knew this was the parish I wanted to serve. I guess God always gets you in the end.

Embarking upon a ministry that is the culmination of a lifelong love affair with the parish that has nurtured them creates Ordained Local Ministry characteristics. One is that many OLM candidates come to ordination in their senior years. For some, the choice to be an OLM was made for them. The Church would simply not commit itself to the expense of another kind of training for a more 'mobile' priestly career in their retirement years. For others, ordination of any kind has, for most of their lives, not been a possibility because they are women.

When I looked at the possibilities for ordination, the OLM was the only one open to me because of my age and because for most of my life the priesthood has not been open to women. I think that if I had been younger I might have liked to train for stipendiary ministry.

The offer of Ordained Local Ministry training for priesthood is no longer quite Hobson's choice in the way that it is described here. Certainly there remains an age discrepancy that might eliminate a candidate for training as a stipendiary or Non-Stipendiary Minister (NSM), but it seems that the growth of locally ordained ministries in many places, and the respect accorded within a wider understanding of priesthood, has enabled more to opt positively for the local position. If the sample of students in the previous chapter and those clergy in this one might be repeated on a larger scale, we will see that the average age of those now opting for the Ordained Local Ministry route is slightly younger. Those interviewed from the training programme had an average age of about 55. Those in this chapter averaged between 65 and 70. None of the students described opting for the Ordained Local Ministry training route as anything other than a positive choice from among other positive possibilities. Training as an OLM is not simply something to offer church members who are entering retirement and whom the incumbent would like to see usefully deployed. However, it should be noted that in a Church that is increasingly obsessed with its less than youthful look within the pews, Ordained Local Ministry is a positive statement to be making about those in senior years.

Ordained Local Ministry: a complementary ministry?

The advantages of a localized priesthood are easy to see. The candidates are established within their communities, can only proceed with the assent and support of those communities, and arrive as clergy as a very well-known quantity. There is a sense in which they do not have to explain who they are, and the basic knowledge of where everything is in both parish community and church community will usually be a given. There is no sense, then, of starting from scratch. Furthermore, OLMs avoid the disruptions of moving house or living in a property that is owned and maintained by the Church. For the cynical, this will seem to be something of a denial of the element of sacrificial living that some see as part and parcel of the priestly calling. But physical relocation can also be seen as a relative freedom. There are times when things go wrong, and even if such moments are faced and dealt with, most clergy can eventually make a fresh start again in another place. The opportunity to 'move on' in that sense simply does not exist for the OLM. At first sight this appears to be a disadvantage. Nobody likes to face up to their ghosts, but most might agree that there is something humanly creditable about doing so. A gospel of reconciliation and forgiveness is not worth much if proclaimed but not lived. OLMs have always to live with no other choice than that. Their communities know them, 'warts and all':

> There is what seems to be a downward side of everyone having known me for so long. If you have any personal 'baggage', like your kids have been up on a drugs charge or you have been divorced, then everyone knows about it and you have to live with that quite publicly, knowing that you can't just move away. The same as if you fall out with people of the parish. You have to stay and deal with it because you are just there.

Such sacrificial staying put offers an example to all clergy, and is thus an important element in the relationships between different kinds of clergy – and the local strand of ordained ministry was seen by the OLMs as necessarily existing only in partnership with the other types:

I think that you need a balance of all three ordained ministries within the wider Church. There is a sense in which I opted for OLM because it suited me and I recognize OLM as a particular strand of ordained ministry, but it is one that would be lost without the other two. OLM has worked for me because I have been able to draw on a lifetime of local experience and channel it into a local ministry precisely because I am working with the familiar. It needs a balance. Stipendiary and NSM clergy bring a freshness with a new look at things. OLMs bring stability because they know the people with whom they have often grown up and have come to know and trust because of this. I have seen how OLMs can enhance parish life because they provide a complementary ministry.

Others expanded on this as a feature that enabled gifts to grow and be well used in the busy world of parish ministry. 'Administration' has come to be regarded as something of a tedious necessity in parish life and one that we blame for getting in the way of what we perceive and name as positive pastoral practices. When I was a curate, I used to afford myself time to visit parishioners and members of the congregation I served. I liked doing it. I remember my vicar one day commenting to me that he appreciated me doing it and wishing that he had the time to do the same. 'When they see me coming now, they know it's terminal,' he lamented. The business of managing the church plant and the quantities of paperwork in a parish where there is no money to pay for secretarial help has made administration the dirty word it is today. Yet 'administer' has the same root as the word 'minister', and perhaps a better theology of ministry might enable us to feel more positive about administration. In that sense the presence of an OLM on a ministry team can afford space and time for managing and for coming to see good administration as no less pastoral than the hospital visit or casual call – pastoral work for which the OLM is therefore set free:

> I was in senior management in my career and very aware that what others did you sometimes had to sort out. There is a sense in which I now feel freer to do the kinds of things that allow me to spend time with people face to face. All of this is because I neither have the same levels of paperwork as before, nor the overall responsibility for the running of the parish, which can be time-consuming.

The development of complementary ministry must, then, enable the growth of complementary gifts. These in turn can allow the work of what has hitherto been seen as undeniably pastoral ministry (such as visiting the sick) to be in partnership with those less obvious features (such as care of buildings). Administration then gains a sense of being 'towards ministry' in a way that visiting already is.

There are difficulties in serving as an OLM in the parish, and good and regular communication between different members of ministry teams is needed to deal with them. While all agreed that a familiar figure could give some security and a sense of stability in a parish community, there were instances where some had experienced a manipulation of that familiarity:

> During the vacancy people would get disgruntled over things and would come to me because they knew me well. The risk was that I might become a kind of go-between, and it is easy to see how this might happen with a new incumbent in the parish. People come to you if they have a problem with her and they expect you to deal with it, and it is really an attempt to divide loyalties which, while I think it is not unique to the OLM/incumbent relationship, it is fairly particular to it because we are around all the time.

The other obvious risk and disadvantage is that the OLM might simply be taken for granted. Having always been there as the face of consistency, some OLMs described the experience of having to manage long periods without an incumbent, something that they had not anticipated:

> There is no payment for what we do, so you give a lot of yourself and your time at your own expense and I don't mind that, but sometimes I wonder if that is really appreciated. I felt that most during the period when we were last between vicars.

Ordained Local Ministry: a paradox of change

The OLM is not so very new. As already noted, it looks as though that was the model under which the churches that Paul founded and described in the New Testament were fashioned. The apostolic ministry was the roving managerial ministry style adopted by Paul. However, the churches that he and others founded were administered by local men and women. The emergence of the presbyters as the church grew and developed saw this continue.

The irony for these locally adopted 'ministers' is that, as figures of consistency, they watched over phenomenal degrees of change. The same might be said of the OLM, as we have them at the moment. Figures of continuity – and perhaps adopted by their congregations as the familiar faces of 'unchangingness' – they are in fact often the catalysts for change. Most of those interviewed for this chapter could see and appreciate this irony. It is, however, an awesome responsibility and one that requires OLMs to be assured of their value and worth as priests and deacons. They not only need to be clear about who they are, they need to be comfortable with the ways in which others understand them.

As was the case with the students in Chapter 9, central to this is the relationship with the incumbent of the parish and with that incumbent's understanding of who they are and how they operate as OLMs. Most of those involved in this research had the experience of serving with more than one incumbent. For most, the transition had been well managed. The new man or woman had appreciated from the outset that an OLM was on the staff and appeared happy that they would bring a knowledge of the people and place that it would take the newly arrived priest a long time to acquire. Some OLMs described a sense of responsibility for seeing a good ending of one incumbency and a good beginning of the next. In this sense, the OLM sees through a kind of death and birth experience in which they are both undertaker and midwife:

> My first incumbent saw me through to ordination and left a year afterwards. He was great and supportive and encouraged me through the course. Then the new one arrived and we get on well too. He is very inclusive of me and we are able to support each other. He knew that I was part of the parish deal when he came to look at the place and I was on the interview panel and was able to spend some time with him alone as part of the process. That was good because I felt that there was a kind of continuity between the departing incumbent and the new one arriving.

This is a ministry of managing change, and it is one that goes on as the new incumbent begins to feel their way in a new environment. OLMs saw the value in not finding themselves wedded to a tradition that was not open to movement, and they understood the danger of a congregation that interpreted continuity as inflexibility. An awareness of how things got done in the parish community was then not to be regarded as the way in which things would always be done or the way in which the new incumbent should 'learn' to do them. Instead, some OLMs often saw themselves as both guardians of the local tradition and as the key with which those local traditions might be developed. It was important there-fore to develop a good understanding with the incumbent without running the risk of being felt to be in competition with him or her:

> In many ways I think that the new incumbent finds it quite help-ful to have someone like me in place, but sometimes I wonder if he feels slightly threatened by my presence, and I can see that it does make him much more vulnerable. The congregation knows me and I know how we do things, and also incumbents tend to be very different from each other in character and ministry style. It takes people time to adjust and not expect the incumbent to do things like the last one. That is where I think that an OLM can make the difference in that we are seen as a bit of continuity in periods of change. I also try to take a long view of things. Things are bound to be different with a new incumbent at the helm, but that is where I think that I can help people see things in a different way.

By the same token, an incumbent who values the difference an OLM might make will most likely look to enable a sense of part-nership in ministry together by trusting themselves to the greater experience of the OLM in that local context:

> What I really appreciate is that he often comes to me and says that because I have been here for a long time, what are my thoughts on this or that, or how to approach something or tackle a certain person. And the relationship is sufficiently open that I can, when we are on our own, feed back to him how a meeting or some event has gone.

> What I like about her is that she has quickly read my strengths and weaknesses and helps me build on the one and strengthen the other. So we haven't had problems in that sense ourselves, but I am very aware that this is not always the case for other OLMs.

Although the OLM is supposedly called out of the congregation and affirmed by the congregation, there remains the risk of change both for the priest and for the congregation's perception of the priest. We looked at some of this in the previous chapter. For many of the OLMs, the humanness of what it was to be a priest was better preserved precisely because they remained a known quan-tity to the people that they served. Every priest interviewed expressed feeling a confidence in them enjoyed by their congregation. Some sensed that a lot was invested in them as a priest whom the congregation had chosen from among themselves:

> They were very good at affirming what I felt was my calling to ordination. I went to them and said that this was what I felt I was called to do and I can't remember anyone else in all my time here being called out from this congregation for ordination. So I went to the PCC and they were quite happy to affirm that. I think that they have viewed this as one of us becoming one of them. This has always been a sort of working-class type parish and I think that they often see the clergy as people who are above them, and particularly the older members of the congregation. So when this happened to me, for many of them, it was as though one of their own had made it and I think that they were very pleased.

A few of the women clergy experienced a small number of church members reacting to their ordination because they were women. In one case the members merely absented themselves on days when she was around. In another, the experience of having a woman called to ordination, who also happened to be their friend, challenged them to find different ways of looking at the issue of women and ordination and how it made them feel. Here again, the locally discerned vocation to ordination becomes, for some, an effective catalyst for change.

That local challenge to change, and to shape new insights into priesthood, has affected the wider Church. So, the once held perception of the priest being sent by the bishop to serve anywhere at any time has evolved in the reformed traditions into something different. It has seen full-time paid clergy responding to advertisements for new posts, taking account of housing and schools, and attending competitive interviews in discerning where they might serve next. It has seen the advent of the priest worker in the form of non-stipendiary ministry and a fuller understanding of what it means to be a priest in the workplace. It is an evolution that continues now in the challenge to understand and value Ordained Local Ministry as a distinct dimension of what it means to be called to serve the Church as a priest. While all clergy might receive the same ordination, this distinctiveness needs to be noted and affirmed. Some had stories of colleagues who had been advised that in the event of their circumstances changing and their having to move home, they might be 'upgraded' to non-stipendiary ministry. What does that mean? What does it say about commitment to a particular vision of priesthood? Is there a different grading or is this part of a mindset about an inherited view of priesthood that is unable to change or see new dimensions to it?

There is, I think, a deeply held concern that any change in our understanding of what it means to be a priest somehow weakens it. Some years ago there was a flurry of correspondence in a leading Catholic journal responding to an article in which the author had made the suggestion that the call to priesthood might not be a life-time call for some. It might, instead, be a calling that came for part of a person's life before they moved on to express their Christian vocation in another way. There was, he argued, some scriptural support for this idea. Some of the prophets seem to have fulfilled their calling like that. Amos seems to have been some kind of horticulturalist before his call to prophecy and may well have returned to it afterwards. The response to his suggestion that the Church consider this as a new perception of what it might mean to live as a priest was an avalanche of protest and criticism.

What we have in the unique experience of the OLM is a challenge in which we are invited not only to get to grips with the notion of a call to local priesthood, but also to ponder seriously the implications of that experience. Notions of priesthood should not be reduced to theoretical concepts. This is not a debate in the abstract about the validity of the Ordained Local Ministry status, but rather a consideration of how OLMs have been received during the last ten years of their existence.

What we find in considering that experience is that the closer to the grassroots of the Church one goes, the more affirming the reaction to the experience. With few exceptions, the local church community was well able to come to terms with this changed perception of what it meant to be a priest. Much of this was due to the involvement of the congregation from the beginning and the way in which the training process engaged them. Here indeed was 'one of their own', and they were not only affirming of the person, but saw their ordination as no less an ordination than that of their incumbent or other clergy:

I haven't felt that they treat me any differently at my church. We have a new deacon who is stipendiary and we do things together. I guess we know what our differences are and that he will eventually move on, but I am clear that it is part of my calling to stay. I feel that I am called to be a priest and that I am called to serve a place as well. So the categories of priest might be different, but they shouldn't be seen as higher or lower. It is just different. God has called all of us.

Experience of Ordained Local Ministry is now fairly widespread in parts of the Church, but the Scheme is still in its infancy and needs more time for greater understanding of ordination to a locality to percolate through the upper levels of the Church:

> Ten years is still a short period of time to get established and for everyone to work through what kind of impact OLM might have made in parish life. To do that without people feeling frightened or threatened is bound to take a bit of time. It is not about being better in ministry; it is about working with other forms of ministry. Our ordination is the same as any other priest. It is just that we have made a commitment to express that priestly ministry within a particular congregation or group of congregations.

If the laity at local level had felt Ordained Local Ministry to be the positive face of priesthood, there were also some clergy who were either unsure of their status or who didn't really understand the concept of, and commitment to, locally expressed ordained ministry:

> I think that some OLMs do feel they are bottom of the pile and I saw an example of this the other day at a meeting I attended. Huge distinctions were being made, and even the NSMs came out saying that they had been made to feel a bit second class – so how were we supposed to feel? So the categorizing is not really helpful. There are many who see OLM as an easy way to get ordained, but I am afraid that I don't think that it is.

Many of the OLM candidates and the OLM clergy openly admitted their disinclination towards academic study. Some lamented the change towards a more academic style as possibly excluding or discouraging potential candidates who might make very good priests, but not get very good degrees. Some OLMs were able to rationalize the importance of the style of training that they had undergone, and see it as a change in educational preparation for a changed ministry style. There was a confidence for most that this was right for them. But there were some who, despite all this, found themselves harbouring a nagging doubt as to their pedigree in the company of their clergy colleagues who held university degrees:

> I am slightly in awe of clergy who have had an academic training where they have done in-depth study and know about biblical scholarship, and I know I have had a lot of life experiences and that I am quite competent in that way, but in the academic knowledge side I feel that there is a gap for me.

A change in training for a change in ministry style

The gap that the priest in the above quote feels perhaps demands some reflection on the changes that the training programme has undergone in recent years. For many it is the most significant change that they have had to face, and it was clear from the interviews at this point that the clergy had different views and were still adapting to the changes that the course had adopted. The Ordained Local Ministry course as it now stands is accredited by the University of Bangor, which offers the participants a diploma at the end of their course with the opportunity to translate that into a degree following the completion of further modules. The students interviewed in Chapter 9 had mixed feelings about the change in emphasis, though most felt positive. Some of the clergy who had been directly affected by the changes remembered feeling anxious:

> The training was fine, but I was concerned and nervous when the course became somewhat more academic because that is not where my strengths are. It really worried me because it was very daunting and I had a very testing time. The course staff were very supportive, but if I had known that the course was going to change like that, I would probably not have done it and I think that people like me with no academic background might well be put off being able to put their call into action.

Others felt that it was a change in the wrong direction, not because they found the rigours of academic life daunting, but because they felt it was a dismantling of the essential characteristics for a training programme fitting a practical context:

> I think that the course went a long way to equip us for Ordained Local Ministry because a lot was geared to the parish setting and we were obliged to apply it to that context. There are some who think that all training for ministry should go this way. It was all very well having the theory, but how did you apply it? That was where OLM training had the edge.

Some of the older clergy were glad to have trained before the shift in training emphasis and style had been adopted, fearing that they might not have coped with it in its new form:

> If I am quite honest, all in all, I am quite glad that it was as it was when I trained, with a strong bias towards the practical and the experiential.

For others, a defined practical nature to the training programme simply allowed them to complete a training that had begun for them in the University of Life:

> When I first floated the idea of ordination, the chief worry of some of the church members was how I would cope with addressing a large group such as a congregation. That was not the problem. I did that most days at work. What my training did was to show me how. The OLM course seemed to complement the life experience and work experience I was having.

Some greatly appreciated the changes, finding them both unexpected and challenging because they raised things that the University of Life had not brought to their attention:

> What the training did was to get me thinking more about the Bible in a different and, I think, deeper way. It faced me with things that I would never have been confronted with, like cloning and stem cell research. I had never thought deeply about where I stood on subjects like that.

So it is clear that there is no consensus on the merits of the changes themselves. However, managing the changes of training for a new variant of priesthood coheres with the requirement that any priest must be prepared for the changes. The creation of more diversity and opportunity in training is part of a necessary commitment to manage change. The course, like the candidate, and like the priest it turns out at the end, while remaining faithful to the original vision (itself a significant change in understanding priestly function), must recognize that part of that vision is to enable positive change in a Church that often struggles with any change at all.

OLMs as instruments of change

For a millennium and a half, the Church managed to run itself without the seminary-styled training dreamed up by Cardinal Pole and augmented by the Council of Trent.[3] Since that time, the purpose of such a training has been a perennial question that has never been answered with real satisfaction. Furthermore, it has within the last 50 years been a style of training that has had to compete alongside other emerging training ideologies. As long ago as 1821, the Austrian Chancellery posed itself the question as to the true worth and value of residential training and answered it in the following way:

In the history of the Church there have been many fine priests and bishops who never attended a seminary. Yet they are useful. Experience shows that the vocation of candidates is neither quite pure nor quite resolute. They have worldly motives mixed with ideals. Their vocation has to be purified and strengthened.[4]

If the purpose of ordination training is to purify and strengthen what is already being called out of a man or woman, is it possible to discern these criteria in Ordained Local Ministry training and the priests who emerge as a result of it? I think so, for it seems to me that the inception of Ordained Local Ministry Schemes to train clergy locally reminds us quite pointedly that ordination is not just about the individual called to be a priest or deacon: it is also about a strengthening and purifying of the community each is called to serve. Perhaps the one can be an effective sign to, and enabler of, the other?

The call to exercise a priestly vocation as OLMs demands, as we have seen, not only a developed sense of community, but a sacrificial commitment to it. This would seem to be the chief strength of the Ordained Local Ministry course as it has evolved, and was the characteristic of it that all of those interviewed were most drawn by and admiring of. The value of being in community not only supported them in their sponsoring congregations, but enabled them to grow as a student community through their learning:

> To study and work quite closely with a varied group of people from quite different backgrounds over three years saw us grow quite close in that time. We would often work on the assignments together and talk them through on the phone together. That kind of contact was invaluable.

If the OLMs have learned nothing else, then they will be abundantly clear that they, in their local communities, are being watched by other parts of a wider Church: one discerning whether this is a viable way forward for the ordained ministry of the Church of God as it faces considerable change. They are already instruments of change in that they stand as a living sign of a slightly altered perception of the priestly tradition. Many of them are instruments of change within the parishes that they serve by the way that they are able to encourage church members to be positive about a new incumbent and the way that he or she might lead the community. In all of this, as I listened to them tell me about their training and life as OLMs in the parishes they served, I was given the picture of a priesthood that had been genuinely empowered by the communities that it had returned to serve.

The effect of this was threefold. First, a gradual and emerging confidence both in themselves and in those communities; second, a sense of real partnership in ministry; and third, some radically altered perceptions caused by them being a sign of change that enabled others to face fear of change in their own way and time:

> I have grown in confidence because of this training. It has come about through what I have learned in the company of the people who have supported me. We learned together. The change that has come about in us is with a growing sense of confidence to work together in God's ministry and mission.

> In one sense, I think I have been a sign of change. While I haven't moved from my parish, I have changed from being a layperson to an ordained one, but only with the consent and support of my congregation. So we have effected that change together and I think that has been the key. Sometimes I think that the ordained ministry used to be seen as imposed upon parishes, but I see this process as committing itself to an ordained ministry that comes up alongside the community it wants to serve.

> There have been some significant changes in our parish and the acceptance of me as a woman and as a priest is one of them. That is not just down to me. We had a marvellous woman priest with us until recently and she provided some good models of ministry that helped to break through some of those perceptions about women. Being in training, with all that going on, has been like the next step. So maybe I feel I have been a bit of an instrument of change as I am one of their own, so to speak. There were some who were quite unsure about the idea of women clergy. They were all very gracious about it, but it was amazing as to how they came to move on the matter. It was wonderful to see. Maybe I had a tiny part in that.

Notes

1 Hinde, Thomas, *A Field Guide to the English Country Parson*, William Heinemann, London, 1984, p. 11.

2 *Crockford's Clerical Directory*, 99th edn, 2006/2007, Church House Publishing, London, 2005.

3 Pole summoned a synod of the Church of England in November 1555. Its decrees first used the term 'seminary', which were later adopted at the Council of Trent in 1563.

4 Chadwick, Owen, 'The Seminary', in Sheils, W. J. and Wood, Diana (eds), *The Ministry: Clerical and Lay*, Blackwell, Oxford, 1989, p. 22.

11. Selecting Ordained Local Ministers

GEOFF MASON

So they proposed two, Joseph called Barsabbas, who was also known as Justus, and Matthias. Then they prayed and said, 'Lord, you know everyone's heart. Show us which one of these two you have chosen to take the place in this ministry and apostleship from which Judas turned aside to go to his own place.' And they cast lots for them, and the lot fell on Matthias; and he was added to the eleven apostles. (Acts 1.23–6)

What a wonderful phrase, it conjures up all sorts of pictures in the mind about nasty substances engulfing the poor man. It does, though, show how call and selection have been important in the life of the Church since the demise of Judas and the selection of Matthias to replace him. The way in which Matthias was selected may be rather different from the present-day selection process for Ordained Local Ministry, but there are important points in common. The apostles prayed and said, 'Lord, you know everyone's heart. Show us which one of these two you have chosen to take the place in this ministry and apostleship' (Acts 1. 24–5). The selection process for Ordained Local Ministry is rooted in prayer at every stage: in the parish, at the selection conference, and not least in the life of the candidate. Canon John Whitelam, the late well-loved, conscientious and slightly eccentric priest at St Agnes, Kennington, one of the original 'Brandon' parishes, adopted a similar process to that recounted in the Acts of the Apostles. He asked for nominations from the congregation, for men to be put forward for selection as OLMs. He then placed the nominations in the tabernacle, next to the Blessed Sacrament, for it was a traditional Anglo-Catholic parish. The following week was to be spent in prayer, the nomination papers were then removed, and the congregation voted. Two men were put forward and were duly interviewed by the then Bishop of Woolwich, the Right Reverend Michael Marshall. It was quite a relaxed affair, but the Bishop turned down one of them as he lived several miles from

Kennington and, although a regular communicant, he could not be seen as part of the local community. The other, Sonny Brown, an ex-soldier who is now a Chelsea Pensioner, was a much-loved member of the congregation who went on to exercise a valued priestly ministry spanning three decades. The selection process for Ordained Local Ministry has changed considerably, but as we read further, we will see common themes from both of the above processes recurring in what is happening today.

Make no mistake about it, the selection of OLM candidates is a rigorous process. People are being ordained to a ministry for which their licence is local, yet they are ordained as priests within the catholic Church, and this link between catholic and local is important in the context of selection. So let us first look at the way in which a call to be an OLM might arise: 'It is a mark of Ordained Local Ministry that candidates should have been invited by the local church to set out on the path towards ordination.'[1] Exactly how that invitation arises can vary from parish to parish. In fact, the word 'invitation' may not now be appropriate in all cases, although it was initially thought that vocations would come forward solely through the call of the congregation. The reality is that in some cases this is true, but sometimes the impetus for the call will come from the incumbent, and on occasions candidates will indicate that they feel called to this pattern of ministry. What is essential is that if the call is an external one – that is, from the congregation – then the candidate must be able to internalize it and own it for himself/herself. Similarly, if a person puts himself or herself forward, then the congregation needs to be fully supportive of that call. In a recent survey, the question was asked of a number of OLMs, 'How did you come to recognize that *God* wanted you to be a priest?'[2] Of those who answered the question, 26 mentioned a personal theme, 19 said 'the vicar' and 40 said 'the congregation'. In the Diocese of Southwark, all candidates who are exploring their call to any pattern of accredited ministry are required to attend a Vocations Guidance Unit. Here, with others on the same journey, they spend a day looking at the nature of call and at the theology of vocation, before returning to their parishes for further discussion with their incumbent. At a later stage, a Director of Ordinands will visit the PCC to ensure that they, on behalf of the congregation, acclaim the candidate and would wish to accept his/her ministry in the parish, should they be ordained. The vote taken has to be almost unanimous. Experience shows that PCCs take this responsibility very seriously and a number of candidates have not been put forward at this stage, or have been told to develop further in certain areas. The role of the local church in encouraging and discerning the gifts of people for leadership roles is given a prominent place in the New Testament. This is highlighted in an Advisory Council for the Church's Ministry publication, *Call to Order*: 'God's call comes to the church as community and to individuals as part of the community. The community having determined its own special needs will seek from among its members those with the appropriate gifts of character and skill to meet the needs and match the opportunities.'[3]

The visit of a Director of Ordinands to a parish is not just to ascertain the level of congregational support for a candidate. In the case of Ordained Local Ministry, the parish itself has also to be selected. The parish needs to show that there is a pattern of shared ministry in place or a commitment to it. The ideal setting for an Ordained Local Ministry is among a team of people, which can be manifest in a ministry team, although it is recognized that a wider variety of informal teams and patterns of shared ministry exist within a diocese. Reality shows that it is often the emergence of a prospective OLM that encourages such structures to be put in place. It is, however, important that this does happen, as there have been cases of OLMs left isolated during an interregnum or an incumbent's illness. In one such parish, there was collusion between the congregation and the OLM. The OLM felt quite flattered to be put in the place of an incumbent for several months, and the congregation were quite content to dump an unreasonable workload on him. After a relatively short period of time, the OLM was under considerable pressure and reacted accordingly with impatience and irritation, which then led to frustration and anger among the congregation.

The PCC has to pass a resolution stating that it will set up a support group for an OLM candidate during training. This group will, with others as needed, join with the candidate in those training modules that take place within the parish. They also prepare a parish profile, which is sent to Bishops' Selection Advisers (formerly selectors) prior to attendance at a Bishops' Advisory Panel (formerly Selection Conference), showing the context in which the candidate's ministry will be set. A provisional job description that is 'not cast in stone' indicates that the parish have given thought to the possible ministry that an OLM might exercise. This is quite important, for I remember a very angry and frustrated Reader coming for an interview in the days when I was a rural dean. She had recently been licensed, and had gone back to her parish where nobody had thought what role she might have or what her ministry might be. It was with much sadness that she had to move to another church in order to fulfil her ministry. As this illustrates, the relationship between congregation, incumbent and candidate is crucial, and that is why it is essential that the parish context is looked at seriously.

Candidates for Ordained Local Ministry will be at least 30 years of age and normally no more than 60 at the time of attending a Bishops' Advisory Panel. They will be established members of their congregation and will have worshipped there for three years or more. It is important that an OLM candidate has a good knowledge of the wider community and a commitment to it. This means that they will live in the area or within easy reach of it. There must also be an intention to continue living there for a considerable period of time, though one recognizes that unforeseen circumstances such as redundancy or redeployment might occur. Ministering in the same parish over a number of years means that OLMs have to exhibit a maturity that will enable them to work effectively with different incumbents. This requires adaptability to change and being able to embrace new ideas.

During an interregnum, OLMs may find themselves in a more prominent role liturgically, and then, with the appointment of a new incumbent, need to step 'backwards' a couple of paces. For some this comes as a relief, and for others it can be quite painful, so Diocesan Directors of Ordinands once again will be looking for maturity and self-awareness in candidates. The situations and qualities described above may be requirements for all patterns of ministry, but are especially so in the case of OLMs.

A Director of Ordinands will interview OLM candidates on four or five occasions. The criteria on which a candidate is interviewed are the same as those for stipendiary/non-stipendiary ordinands. They include:

1 *Personal history and background*: significant and formative events that have shaped the life of the candidate and their effect; occupational pattern.
2 *Development of faith*: when and how the candidate's faith became important to them; ability to understand that faith and communicate it.
3 *Development of a sense of vocation*: detailed reflection on the candidate's vocational journey; how did it start and what have been the catalysts?
4 *Church involvement and experience*: churches they have attended, past and present; their involvement in church life; ability to reflect on different models of mission and ministry that they have experienced.

5 *Leadership and collaboration*: the candidate's preferred style of leadership; ability to motivate and work alongside others.

6 *Personality and character, including leisure and voluntary activities*: strengths and weaknesses, self-awareness, evidence of maturity and being able to cope with the demands and pressures of ordained ministry.

7 *Spiritual development and practice*: the candidate's prayer life; how do they experience the presence of God? Have they reflected on their spiritual life with a mentor/soul friend/ spiritual director?

8 *Personal relationships including domestic situation*: if the candidate is single, the need for a candidate to have considered what kind of relationships they need to sustain them in ministry. If married, the need to ensure that the spouse and family are supportive of the candidate's vocation. The need to be able to live within the guidelines of *Issues in Human Sexuality*.[4]

9 *Quality of mind*: an ability to reflect theologically and make connections between faith and life; openness of mind; potential to undertake a course of theological training.

10 *Mission and evangelism*: the candidate's experience of mission and evangelism and ability to reflect on it; does the call to mission permeate a candidate's thinking, prayer and action?[5]

If the candidate is married, then a meeting is arranged during the discernment process between a Director of Ordinands and the candidate's spouse. This is not a test for the spouse to pass. It is to ensure that there is family support for the candidate should they start training and eventually be ordained. The spouse needs to be aware of the commitment required by an ordinand during training and of the change in role after ordination. There is a cost to priestly ministry, and particular issues to be faced where someone has been a layperson in the parish where he or she is to be ordained.

A Director of Ordinands then writes a report on the candidate based on the series of interviews. If everything has gone smoothly, the visit by a Director of Ordinands to the PCC, which has already been referred to, will take place. In the Diocese of Southwark, a candidate would then meet with an 'Examining Panel' rather than an individual Examining Chaplain, as other candidates for ordained ministry do. The purpose of this is to give the bishop a second opinion before he sponsors a candidate to attend a Bishops' Advisory Panel. The Examining Panel comprises three people, who are usually Examining Chaplains, and who take on the roles that Bishops' Selection Advisers would at a Bishops' Advisory

Panel. One of them looks particularly at church involvement, vocation, spirituality and faith; another at pastoral experience, self-
awareness and relationships; and the third concentrates on quality
of mind and potential for training. It has proved a very useful
exercise, particularly for those candidates who have little experience of interviews. During the selection process, references have
been collected, and an enhanced criminal disclosure form, ethnic
monitoring form and Statement of Financial Position form have
been completed.

If everybody is happy about the way things are going – and it is
not nearly so daunting as it sounds – then the Diocesan Bishop is
asked if he is willing to sponsor the candidate to attend a Bishops'
Advisory Panel. The important thing to remember is that when
candidates first come forward they do not necessarily fulfil all the
criteria talked about earlier, and quite often – where there is potential – the Diocesan Director of Ordinands will suggest areas where
the candidate might get experience. For example, some candidates
have not studied any theology, or have minimal experience of
formal academic study. Quite a number have not written an essay
for many years, and studying for the Bishop of Southwark's
Certificate in Biblical and Theological Studies over a year can give
them real confidence and a thirst for the subject. Similarly, some
may need to gain more pastoral experience, develop their spiritual
life, or become more self-aware.

Since 1992, when the first Ordained Local Ministry Selection
Conference for candidates from Southwark took place, the confer-
ences have been held on a diocesan basis. They followed the same
pattern as National Selection Conferences for Stipendiary/Non-
Stipendiary ministry, with some exceptions. Where six selectors
were required at a conference, four of them would be Bishops'
Selectors from the diocese, and two from other dioceses. A
Ministry Division Selection Secretary would staff the conference.
Another feature was that a Diocesan Director of Ordinands would
meet with selectors immediately prior to the conference in order to
answer any questions concerning parishes, candidates, or training
scheme. These were valuable meetings, particularly when it came
to briefing selectors from other dioceses. Candidates were also able
to present topics of concern or interest for discussion that reflected
their local context. The conferences were rigorous, but it was considered vital for them to be as accessible as the subsequent training
would be: accessible for people with little formal academic
training, and from a rich variety of cultures and occupations. This
proved to be successful, and in recent years over 20 per cent of
candidates have been minority ethnic candidates, and there has

been a strong representation of candidates (over 30 per cent) from Urban Priority Area parishes. It is *Ordained Local Ministry* that selection is for, and while skills learned in training may be transferable, understanding the context for ministry is vital. It does not take too much imagination to understand that a person from a wealthy suburb in the outer part of a diocese like Southwark might find it difficult to minister in Brixton and vice versa.

Recently, diocesan Ordained Local Ministry Selection Conferences have been scrapped, and all OLM candidates will in future attend National Bishops' Advisory Panels. It has also been stated that Diocesan Directors of Ordinands will not meet with Bishops' Selection Advisers prior to panels, as this is not a good use of their time. It is clear that some dioceses do not have enough candidates to make their own panel viable, but the answer could be for dioceses to work together, as did Southwark, Canterbury and Salisbury recently. It was an occasion when three selectors grilled the Diocesan Directors of Ordinands for over one and a half hours about context and training schemes. At a recent National Selection Conference, a Selection Secretary and a selector were heard by an OLM candidate talking disparagingly about Ordained Local Ministry. Until it becomes nationally accepted and understood, there is a need for Bishops' Selection Advisers and staff to have firsthand experience of Ordained Local Ministry. The importance of diocesan Bishops' Advisory Panels just for Ordained Local Ministry was highlighted for me a good number of years ago. One selector from a rural diocese, where the notion of a multicultural context may well have been limited or quite different, spoke of her difficulty in understanding the regional accent of one candidate from the inner city. We were able to put the selector's mind at rest by saying that the parish from which he came did not have a problem with this. (It might even have been the case that the regional accent of the selector could have posed the same problem for the candidate and his parish!) It would be a great pity if Ordained Local Ministry were to follow NSM and become a pattern of ministry for middle-class professionals. Let us not forget that Ordained Local Ministry was given a considerable boost by the report *Faith in the City*,[6] only 20 years ago, and much has been accomplished since. It was important for Diocesan Directors of Ordinands to be able to meet Selection Advisers and answer questions about candidates' contexts, and it would be useful if this practice were to continue.

You might guess from all this that there are changes happening on the Selection Conference front. A Selection Conference is now called a Bishops' Advisory Panel and a selector is referred to as a

Bishops' Selection Adviser. The Selection Secretary who administers the panel is now known as a Bishops' Advisory Panel Secretary. Thus the terms 'selectors' and 'Selection Conferences' in this chapter refer to events pre-July 2005. It is good to see that 'cognitive testing' introduced in 1995 is no longer used. While cognitive testing can have value, the high-level verbal reasoning test was very difficult for those whose second language is English. Ministry Division do not have statistics that confirm this, but the reports from Selection Conferences received in Southwark would do so. This exercise, although used to 'count people in', and thought to help those with little formal academic qualifications, could be a confidence shaker at the start of a conference. The Bishops' Advisory Panels for Ordained Local Ministry, NSM and stipendiary candidates will now run from Monday to Wednesday and, instead of cognitive testing, each candidate will now make a presentation of his or her own choice; and instead of the Bishops' Advisory Panels for Ordained Local Ministry meeting over weekends, which was helpful to people whose jobs gave them little opportunity to take days off, they will meet from Monday to Wednesday as panels for NSM and stipendiary candidates do now. As before, there will be three individual interviews, a written exercise and a group exercise.

The thing that really impresses candidates is the way in which prayer is at the heart of a Bishops' Advisory Panel. It takes us back to the 'lot falling on Matthias' and the call to Sonny Brown in Kennington. There is no doubt that Bishops' Selection Advisers and staff do their best to create a prayerful and convivial atmosphere at conferences. Following the conference, a report is sent to the Diocesan Bishop stating whether or not the Bishops' Selection Advisers recommend the candidate for training and whether there are any conditions made alongside the recommendation. Occasionally this may be something in the nature of 'subject to a full review after the first year of training'. If the Diocesan Bishop accepts the recommendation of the Bishops' Selection Advisers, he then writes to the candidate outlining the result of the panel and asking the candidate to contact the Director of Ordinands, who will then show him or her the report and discuss it in detail.

When the 'lot' did not fall on Joseph called Barabbas who was surnamed Justus, it is pretty certain that he was not a very happy man. When a candidate is not recommended for training on the Ordained Local Ministry Scheme, emotions can run high. There is a difference between the candidate for Ordained Local Ministry and those for NSM and stipendiary ministry. In the case of Ordained Local Ministry, members of the parish have played quite a part in the selection process, committing themselves – often after much discussion – to a particular style of ministry and setting up a support group. They will also have produced a provisional job description and a parish profile and stated that they would welcome the candidate's ministry. It is common for the congregation and incumbent to show more anger at the non-recommendation than the candidate. Time and conversation are required before any action is taken, and of course the Director of Ordinands is not in a position to share details of the report with the incumbent or congregation. The candidate can feel very exposed dealing with his or her own emotions, and at the same time handling those of the congregation. The Director of Ordinands has an important role here when working through the contents of the report with the candidate and the reasons for the decision of the Bishops' Selection Advisers. Fortunately, the whole of the selection process is now transparent as a result of the Data Protection Act. This means that candidates can now see all of the papers (including references that the panel have at their disposal) and the panel report. As a result, they are able to discuss matters openly and honestly with their incumbent, and this can help the situation in the parish. The candidate can also give permission for the Director of Ordinands to talk with the incumbent and look at appropriate ways of support. It is a very difficult time for a candidate, and most of them will experience all the emotions pertaining to a bereavement. Candidates often describe to me the feelings of anger, sadness, loss, bewilderment and devastation. Counselling is offered to candidates, and it is a time when a first-class Spiritual Director has an important role. We have mentioned both candidate and congregation, but the family are also very much part of the trauma. Time is a healer, and quite often a candidate will return to a Bishops' Advisory Panel at a later date. This, except in very rare circumstances, is not within two years, so that the candidate can work through the painful experience. The important thing is not to rush headlong into training for another ministerial role, but to take time and, above all, to pray about the future.

The reverse is often true for those who are recommended, and fortunately this is the majority of candidates. They are usually delighted, and one has to ground both them and their congregation in reality. The parish have made certain commitments about style of ministry and setting up a support group: easy to talk about, but sometimes harder to put into practice. It is very rare that even in a recommended candidate's Bishops' Advisory Panel report there are not issues to be addressed and weaknesses identified. Let's be honest, none of us is perfect; but in the euphoria following the recommendation, the candidate needs to be brought down to earth and helped to work on those issues. They also have to remember that the recommendation is for training and not for ordination. The hard work is about to start, and the sacrifices required on a training course will have to be made; but it is the continuation of a journey which, thank God, is providing in so many cases a fruitful and enriching ministry, helping to build up the kingdom of God in parishes throughout the diocese.

Notes

1 Advisory Board of Ministry, Policy Paper no. 1, *Local NSM*, Advisory Board of Ministry, London, 1991.

2 *Stranger in the Wings: A Report on Local Non-Stipendiary Ministry*, Advisory Board of Ministry Policy Paper no. 8, Church House Publishing, London, 1998, p. 68.

3 *Call to Order*, Advisory Council for the Church's Ministry, London, 1989, p. 20.

4 *Issues in Human Sexuality: A Statement by the House of Bishops of the General Synod of the Church of England*, Church House Publishing, London, 1991.

5 Notes for Diocesan Directors of Ordinands, Ministry Division, with effect from 2005.

6 *Faith in the City: The Report of the Archbishop's Commission on Urban Priority Areas*, Church House Publishing, London, 1985.

12. Training Ordained Local Ministers

NIGEL GODFREY

Brothers and sisters, join in imitating me, and observe those who live according to the example you have in us. (Philippians 3.17)

Emerging from inspection

During the autumn of 2004, the Southwark Ordained Local Ministry Scheme underwent a Bishops' Inspection, which involved three inspectors examining everything from the educational rationale of the Southwark programme to delivery in the classroom, from administration to how parishes with ordinands experience the programme.

I have been familiar with OFSTED inspections in inner-city schools and know what pressure they place on staff. For me, the Bishops' Inspection was a first-time experience in theological education, so while there was a sense of being put under the microscope, it was a surprisingly pleasant experience with a real feeling that inspectors genuinely wanted to help in the development of the Diocese of Southwark's programme, and they were looking at holes in what we do in a spirit of critical creativity. The report and recommendations have now been published and, thankfully, endorse my optimism! The inspection process is inevitably a time when senior staff associated with the delivery of a programme training ordinands for the diaconate and priesthood are forced to focus on the whole training package. It involves looking at all those questions, which include how, what, which, why and when. Habits die hard and, even worse, sometimes we disconnect what was once a perfectly reasonable exercise from its moorings, so that it now no longer makes any sense. We sometimes need the prompting of an innocent question from an outsider, who arrives not knowing the history of what has gone before, to help us to see the absurdity of a situation. Perhaps the inspectors' report will help us to see some of the spaces and disconnections, as well as recognizing and acknowledging what is creative, coherent and on target. Some of the recommendations highlight developments we were already making, some are for the diocese to consider, and some are demanding thoughtful restructuring and reorganization. But first, a look at the overall national picture of education.

The changing context of education

Education and training are areas of life that are constantly changing. In recent years there has been a vast expansion of higher education in the UK. In the 1960s, expansion produced a large number of new universities and polytechnics, and some experiments with new kinds of institution – such as the Open University. In more recent times there has been growth of existing institutions, whether associated with amalgamation or division to meet the rising numbers entering higher education. Current government targets aim to have 50 per cent of all school leavers entering higher education.

The student profile over the period has changed also, with increasing numbers of women as opportunities have opened up; of mature students, who missed out on higher education first time round; of people returning to education with new career directions in mind; and of migrants looking for qualifications from UK universities. Coupled with this, there has been developing a more sustained culture of lifelong learning, which has meant that many more people generally are regularly returning to education and training.

Over the same period, education has also changed in style, moving from the traditional full-time pattern to an increasing amount of part-time education. The old lecture format has often given way to a more participatory style; many new courses integrate academic studies with fieldwork of various kinds; and it is now possible to combine several disciplines in a single degree. Educational programmes have offered a greater variety of courses and, with increasing amounts of modularization, have made it possible for students to have greater input into their learning programme.

These changes in the national educational programme have to some extent been mirrored in education and training practices associated with ordination training. Residential colleges, catering for full-time training, were joined by non-residential courses offering part-time programmes. The Southwark Ordination Course, established in 1962 by Mervyn Stockwood, moved from being a novelty to being the norm for training. The typical ordinand changed from being young, male and single to being rather older, more likely to be married and, with the ordination of women to the priesthood from 1994 onwards, is just as likely to be female as male. The position nationally is indicated in Table 12.1.

Table 12.1   Ordinands in training (academic year 2002–03)

Training institution		Ordinands		
No.	Type	Total no. per institution type	Average per institution	Percentage male
19	OLM Schemes	217	11	42%
12	Regional courses	586	49	38%
11	Theological colleges*	549	50	68%
42	All institutions	1352	32	51%

* Figures do not include St Michael's College, Llandaff, in Wales, or the Theological Institute for the Scottish Episcopal Church (TISEC).

In recent times, the issue of amalgamation of institutions (either organically or through legal structures) has been explored and is dealt with in the section on regionalization.

What is an Ordained Local Ministry (OLM) Scheme?

The Southwark Ordained Local Ministry Scheme fits into a three-fold national provision associated with the training of people for the ordained ministry in the Church of England. There are residential theological colleges, regional courses and Ordained Local Ministry Schemes.[1] In broad terms, residential colleges train ordinands full time over two or three years, largely for stipendiary ministry. All those under 30 years of age are required to enter by this route. Regional courses train ordinands for stipendiary and non-stipendiary ministry on a part-time basis over three years, with all candidates in this category being over 30; the usual pattern of training is at a central site (or sites) on one evening a week in term time with a number of residential weekends. Ordained Local Ministry Schemes train ordinands over a three-year period exclusively for locally based non-stipendiary ministry. Ordinands are over 30 – indeed, often a good deal older. (The average age on the Southwark Ordained Local Ministry Scheme is 57, which is two years older than the ceiling for those on regional courses. The current range is from 38 to 60.)

The Southwark Scheme had its first intake of ordinands in 1992 and was one of the first four Ordained Local Ministry Schemes to be accredited in the Provinces of York and Canterbury. The experience of these Schemes, which by the time of the publication of *Stranger in the Wings* (published in 1998)[2] were present in a third of the dioceses of England and Wales, exhibited 'considerable diversity in the method, style, context and content of training'.[3] They represent a burgeoning new approach to training that is beginning to make its mark. Despite the great number of Ordained Local Ministry Schemes in England, the number of ordinands training on these programmes is not large in the overall training landscape (16 per cent), though it has been growing annually.

The target group for the Southwark Ordained Local Ministry Scheme are ordinands within the Diocese of Southwark, though with regionalization of training on the way, this and many other things – not least the shape of Ordained Local Ministry training – may change. (The regionalization policy requires the Diocese of Southwark to work with the Dioceses of Canterbury, Rochester and Chichester. Only Southwark and Canterbury have Ordained Local Ministry Schemes at this stage.) OLM ordinands see their vocation as being worked out in their own parish and local context, and in this sense it might be seen as paralleling the Benedictine ideal of stability.[4]

So what makes Ordained Local Ministry training different from other forms of ordination training?

There are three key areas in which the training of OLMs is significantly different from other kinds of training – namely, in the areas of collaborative working, experiential theological learning and its particular approach to integration, and wholeness in the curriculum.

Collaboration

One of the key features is a commitment to collaboration locally of ordained and laypeople. Collaboration on the Southwark Ordained Local Ministry Scheme takes place in two ways: in the parish context, where all selected candidates are required to operate in the context of a ministry team before, during and after training; and in peer groups.

Collaboration: the ministry team

There was an expectation in the early days that ministry teams would be established prior to ordinands being called forth. In some dioceses, the whole ministry team would be the unit of learning, and only at a later stage would an ordinand be drawn out from the group, as is the case in the Diocese of Lincoln. Quite how these ministry teams operate and function depends on the nature and needs of the parish. (The new teams being created for new ordinands in the Diocese of Southwark are to be called 'vocational support teams', a clear emphasis on the need for support and involvement in the training.) The number of participants in the team might vary, but typically there might be between eight and ten members approximately conforming to the ideal size of team according to Meredith Belbin. (Belbin, in his classic *Management Teams: Why They Succeed or Fail*,[5] expressed no surprise that there are 11 people in a cricket or football team.) Southwark's Ordained Local Ministry Scheme contains five major assignments associated with the local context. The level of collaborative participation of the ministry team (or others drawn into the team for the particular assignment question) varies depending on the task.

An example may illustrate this. Ordinands in a module 'Mission in Local Context' are required either to produce a mission statement for their parish or to review the one that their parish already has. Clearly, a good mission statement should give a sense of where a particular parish sees its priorities. The exercise only requires a limited number of words to give the *raison d'être* of the organization, and a brief 'strap-line' to provide an even briefer summary. The exercise may look relatively easy at first glance: a 100-word assignment. But this is the tip of the iceberg. Underneath is the need to get 100 words that are acceptable to the parish as a whole. It raises questions like 'What group with what status will be gathered together in the parish to try and come to some common mind on the subject?' and 'How will this be presented and authorized and/or modified by the PCC?' We can see already that the exercise involves a good deal of planning with a long 'lead-in' time; it might involve questionnaires about how the people in the pews see the priorities; and it has to come up with an agreed statement that can be owned in the parish. Does the statement really speak to them about where they see the mission of the parish, or is it a dead letter gathering dust on a shelf? The ordinand, after hours and hours of work, may have 100 words to show for the assignment, and that accounts for only 5 per cent of the module mark.

The next section of the assignment is also undertaken in the parish and requires the production of a set of objectives for the coming year. This accounts for 10 per cent of the module marks. Again the assumption is made that these objectives will be real and will connect with the mission statement. Unfortunately, many proposed sets of objectives ignore the mission statement. For instance, a mission statement that sees worship and inclusion as vitally important was submitted with a set of objectives that did not even feature ensuring access to the worship space by those with mobility or hearing issues, or the provision of support to those with children.

The objectives also need to be SMART (**S**pecific, **M**easurable, **A**chievable, **R**elevant and **T**ime-based). To be specific, the objective needs to be something that can be easily identified, rather than a generality. To be measurable, it needs to be something quantifiable. To be achievable, there needs to be a real possibility of the target being met. To be relevant, the objectives need to be appropriate to the local community and to match the vision of the church's mission statement. Finally, they need to be time-based. In a year's time, on revisiting the objectives, the parish will need to know what progress has been made towards its target objectives.

A parish that thinks it can put forward the name of an ordinand and can then wash their hands of them and say goodbye for three years, and then expect to get a fully trained deacon at the end, will be very disappointed. Parishes become caught up in their ordinand's training, and as the ordinand is changed through the process, so will the parish be changed too: no pain, no gain.

Collaboration: peer groups

Ordinands study with their colleagues in peer groups of three or four candidates from the same year group. Peer groups are currently re-formed halfway through the course, so that ordinands have the opportunity to work with a variety of colleagues over the period of training. The Scheme believes that it is important for ordinands to produce work collaboratively as this mirrors life in the parish as well as being a sound educational and learning principle. Ordinands produce assignments collectively. Peer group marks can be as high as 50 per cent of the total marks of a module, and candidates receive the same mark as one another regardless of the level of input by particular individuals. This can mean that the peer group can often be very task-oriented. Occasionally, individual needs and the process require the work of a facilitator to bring difficult issues into the open. Lack of attention to these needs can lead to dysfunction and even breakdown, and while this may be a valuable learning experience in its own right it can be painful. Our experience of peer group working has overall been very positive, although some groupings have struggled.

Experiential theological learning

Southwark Ordained Local Ministry Scheme's philosophy of education is based on the need for knowledge to be relevant to local settings so that there can be outcomes in Christian action. This approach parallels the recommendations in the Advisory Board for Ministry (ABM) Ministry Paper no. 4 (1992),[6] where emphasis is given to critical reflection and subsequent action. A key word in the education programme is 'transformation'. Using the thinking of people like Kolb (see Figure 12.1), this has been conceived of as a cycle, where a person explores an activity (gaining a concrete experience), is encouraged to reflect upon it (through reflective observation), then sees how this relates to the theory (abstract conceptualization), and finally moves to taking part in an activity (by active experimentation). The theory suggests that for effective learning to take place there needs to be activity in all four stages. The learning gained by travelling the full cycle brings the person to a new starting point, and therefore it might be perceived as a spiral. An example, using a level 1 (certificate level) module 'New Testament Today', illustrates the process.

Figure 12.1   The Kolb cycle of learning[7]

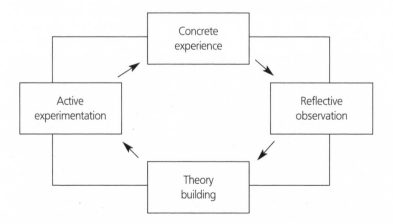

'New Testament Today'

Concrete experience (placement of 60 hours)

The placement might be in a night shelter, a citizens' advice bureau or any community placement the ordinand feels would be helpful to his or her future ministry. Ordinands roll up their sleeves and get involved as volunteers in a way that has been negotiated with the community organization. In advance of the placement, they produce an 'agreement statement' with the placement supervisor, indicating what they hope to learn from the experience in terms of carer, person and minister.

Reflective observation (reflecting on-the-job)

While on the placement, the ordinand is encouraged to reflect on the experience and gain some insights into the nature of ministry through observing, for example, what the stated policy of the organization is and what actually happens on the ground in meeting client needs.

Abstract conceptualization (year group reflection in seminars)

After the placement is completed, ordinands are then encouraged to reflect together as a group on their very different placement experiences and to draw out gospel values they have witnessed in their settings – gospel values that might have been experienced in the most unexpected places. Observations are then integrated into a general reference framework.

Active experimentation (practical working in the home parish)

The last stage in this particular cycle involves the ordinand applying the insights of the placement to their parish setting. Theories might be used as a basis for decision-making and problem-solving.

The learning cycle rarely happens in a simple loop commencing with experience, for learning can take place with entry at different points of the cycle. For example, in the above module, the learning experience begins with input relating to the Gospels. Ordinands explore various approaches to reading the Gospels through a variety of teaching styles from didactic to fully participatory. Before commencing their placement, they undertake two study days exploring with tutors the hinge between the Gospels and the placement. The process is a lot more untidy at the edges than the cycle suggests. More recently, theologians such as Groome and Lartey[8] have modified the cycle to take into account other factors such as the dialogue between 'experience' and the Christian tradition. The challenge of the interface between experience and the Christian tradition is constantly present on the Southwark Ordained Local Ministry Scheme: so in seminars, New Testament study and reflection on placements happen together, not separately.

Walton, in his survey of theological training institutions in the UK,[9] identified seven approaches to such biblical reflection. These range from the most simple connecting of text and situation ('prooftexting') to the rather more sophisticated 'mutual critique' of the experience by the Bible and vice versa. Further study has also been undertaken by Pattison, Thompson and Green, who studied the experience of theological reflection during training among people recently ordained, and the results led them to question whether 'colleges and courses [are] the right place to teach TR [theological reflection] given that it is difficult to provide people with appropriate experiences where TR methods might acquire life and interest'.[10] Ordained Local Ministry Schemes differ from many colleges and courses in their learning process in that they continuously provide such experiences. Many OLM ordinands would regard this as a key strength in the training. Mixed modes of training are now increasingly providing such experiences.

There might be those who would argue that if theological reflection bound up with experience doesn't take place in training, then it is impossible to do anything about it later. (This somewhat disheartening view of clergy may be true.) This points to the importance of trying to get it right at the pre-ordination stage. We also need to recognize that tutors on the Ordained Local Ministry Scheme are not the sole channels of learning, but that learning may occur through exposure to the Church of England in general and one's own parish church in particular. And, of course, ordinands learn from one another.

Integration and wholeness in the curriculum

There is in the Church of England no centrally directed curriculum, though this may change with the regionalization of training and the setting of 'parameters for the curriculum' that might follow the implementation of the Hind report.[11] At the moment, training institutions are required to respond to a number of questions which should enable them to devise appropriate training in the light of their understanding of the Church's mission.[12] The nearest thing at the moment to a directed curriculum is a list of 17 'expectations to be met during Initial Training'.[13] Within these parameters, the aim of the Southwark Ordained Local Ministry Scheme has been one of integration and wholeness. Previously, study units flowed one into another, with subject borders often being blurred and ordinands expected to draw continuously on their cumulative learning in all areas. This was particularly evident in that some subjects that historically might have been considered 'core' to the more traditional training programmes associated with colleges and courses might appear missing – for example, 'doctrine'. It was not that the subject was actually absent, rather that it cropped up through the whole programme. A re-validation of the Scheme in 2001 required that some of these core curriculum areas were made more discrete and explicit in the programme.

In 2002 the Scheme became a partner institution associated with the University of Wales (Bangor) and the programme has been modularized with six 20-credit modules at level 1 and six 20-credit modules at level 2, enabling ordinands to exit at the time of ordination with a diploma (see Figure 12.2). The curriculum moves from 'context' (and text of the tradition) in year 1 to 'Church' in year 2, and 'Mission' in year 3. 'Spirituality' spans the entire three years and deals with liturgy and the interior life. There is then the option to go on to undertake a degree (level 3), with a choice of modules depending on the deacon's/priest's particular interests, and currently half of the students take up this option.

Figure 12.2   The Scheme's programme

The basic diploma programme has used the core material of the old Scheme and reconfigured it into modules that contain a number of elements. An examination of one module will give an insight. Under the old Scheme, the Hebrew Scriptures were a unit with an assignment connected with it in which individual ordinands did an exegesis of a passage from one of the eighth-century BCE prophets and then applied the text to a contemporary setting. Another unit encouraged ordinands to visit the churches of colleagues in their cohort, and in their learning journal to reflect on what they observed. The new module combines these two elements so that a peer group choose a passage together from the eighth-century prophets and undertake an exegesis together. Then as individuals they apply the passage to their own particular context. As a peer group, they arrange to visit each other's churches on a Sunday, and as a group they explore the relationship of what they observe to worship practices in the Hebrew Scriptures. Finally, there follows another individual exercise that asks them to reflect on their visits and, from their observations, to suggest practices that might be adopted in their own setting. These insights they share with their ministry team. Clearly, tact may be required here as change for some parishes can be difficult, and to have their new ordinands suggesting other ways of doing things at such an early stage on the course might ring alarm bells for some!

The module therefore has a number of learning outcomes, not immediately apparent from the basic exercise given. Ordinands are encouraged to work together with others. This involves learning to negotiate, to understand the part that each individual might play, and to relate someone's strengths and weaknesses to the support that they might need. There will be points in the joint assignment where, for the sake of the harmony of the group and the completion of the task, individuals might need to agree to something as a whole that they would find difficult to accept in its parts. There are skills associated with observation and the ability to see in even the worst-ordered parishes something that can be learnt. And there are the rather more obvious skills: for example, applying historical texts to the present while at the same time seeking to understand texts as they have come down to us. In all of this process, ordinands will have been working individually, corporately, centrally and in their parishes.

Throughout the programme, the Scheme has aimed at integration and wholeness in the curriculum, rather than fragmentation. Some Ordained Local Ministry Schemes have resisted connecting to institutions of higher education, despite increasing pressures to do so, in order to avoid what has been described by one Ordained

Local Ministry programme, directed by David Leslie in Liverpool, as 'market driven packages of discrete information'.[14] Ordained Local Ministry Schemes have tried to maintain a holistic approach for which Farley gave the term 'habitus'.[15] Others have since expanded on his idea and, instead of seeing it as an ideal of the past – as perhaps Farley did – have seen it as something to be engaged with in the present.[16]

The Southwark Ordained Local Ministry Scheme has encouraged thinking out of the module or any other 'box', with varying amounts of success, so that sometimes subjects, which on the face of it might look quite discordant, find themselves alongside one another and reacting with others in unexpected ways. An example of this might be 'Doctrine for Today', which has a unit within it exploring other faiths. The assignment that follows requires a Christian doctrine to be seen in the light of the understanding of that doctrine by other faith communities: something very pertinent to the multi-faith society of South London.

The profile of OLM ordinands

The Southwark Ordained Local Ministry Scheme in many ways saw itself as the proud successor of the Southwark Ordination Course (SOC), which was amalgamated to form part of the South East Institute of Theological Education (SEITE) about the time that the Ordained Local Ministry Scheme came to birth. As a symbol of this succession, group photographs of OLM leavers hang on the walls of the diocesan retreat and conference centre at Wychcroft in the leafy countryside of Surrey close to Gatwick airport. The OLM photographs continue where the SOC photographs end, the only difference being that they are now in colour. There are many who mourn the ending of Southwark Ordination Course, for it represented Bishop Mervyn Stockwood's desire to create priest-workers: people working on the factory floor and presiding at the Eucharist; people who would not normally have become priests. There had been a sense, by some, of betrayal as increasingly the Southwark Ordination Course intake became more middle class and the course was perceived as requiring more academic rigour. Some have seen the same process happening with the Southwark Ordained Local Ministry Scheme, so we must now examine the profile of its ordinands.

Gender

Overall, 51 per cent of ordinands in the Church of England are male, but there are differences in the gender ratio of those training through different modes, with only 32 per cent of ordinands at colleges being female, while women outnumber men on regional courses (62 per cent) and Ordained Local Ministry Schemes (59 per cent). For Southwark Ordained Local Ministry Scheme, women represent 63 per cent of ordinands in training, and one current year group has seven women and only one man. (In the very first year (1992) there were seven men and one woman.) Overall, as the numbers are comparatively small, it is difficult to say precisely what the trend might be.

Christian tradition

Residential colleges tend to have ordinands from particular traditions of the Church, and there is only one, Queen's in Birmingham, that has an ecumenical foundation. Regional courses draw from across the Anglican spectrum and have an ecumenical element, with Methodists, members of the United Reformed Church (URC) and people from other Churches training for ministry on them. Ordained Local Ministry Schemes, on the other hand, draw exclusively from the catchment area of the Anglican diocese alone, though with people from parishes in very different traditions: from those associated with 'Reform' to 'Forward in Faith'.[17] What Ordained Local Ministry Schemes lack is an ecumenical dimension. The closest that the Southwark Ordained Local Ministry Scheme comes to one is its ordinands from Local Ecumenical Projects. These are Anglican parishes run in partnership with other denominations, and often with buildings occupied by more than one denomination through a legal sharing arrangement.

Ethnicity

Southwark is the diocese that saw the murder of the black teenager Stephen Lawrence on its streets in 1993, by a white gang that has never been brought to justice. This incident produced the Macpherson Report. The report challenged 'every institution to examine their policies and the outcome of their policies and practices to guard against disadvantaging any section of our communities'.[18] The Diocese of Southwark was one of the first institutions, and certainly the first church institution, to take up the challenge. The diocese engaged Sir Herman Ouseley to investigate institutional racism within the diocesan structures. He reported his findings in 2000.[19] (A follow-up report has been prepared by the diocese to monitor improvements over the intervening period.)

The diocese has made major efforts to try to encourage people from ethnic minorities, so visible in our congregations, to take a more leading role in the Church's leadership. We are still a long way off from having OLMs as a feature of parish life in the Diocese of Southwark fully representative of the diverse people making up the whole community. Attempts to ensure greater inclusion have seen the development of vocation road shows targeting parishes with large ethnic minority congregations. (There are 63 parishes in the Diocese of Southwark that have congregations where more than 60 per cent of attendees are from ethnic minorities. This represents 23 per cent of parishes in the diocese.) The ratio of people from ethnic minorities on Southwark's Ordained Local Ministry Scheme is currently 23 per cent, which is beginning to show signs of being more representative of the Diocese of Southwark as a whole. Some general statistics relating to the Southwark Ordained Local Ministry Scheme are given in Appendix 2.

Academic background

The academic background of ordinands training on the Ordained Local Ministry Scheme appears to be gradually changing. For the first ten years there were significant numbers who were offered academic support tutors: the main reason being that these ordinands had experienced little formal education beyond the age of 15. These individuals came from a variety of backgrounds, including the Caribbean and West Africa as well as indigenous ordinands often from the inner-city or outer-city estates. In contrast to this is the present situation where the array of academic qualifications of OLM ordinands is startling, with only two ordinands not having academic qualifications beyond secondary-school level. Among the ordinands are two with PhDs, four others with higher academic degrees, and the remainder with first degrees, diplomas or certificates in education. What has also become clear is that some ordinands, originally from overseas, have considerable higher education and professional qualifications.

The situation needs to be kept under constant review, and penetrating questions should be asked. Is it the Church institutionally that fails to discern potential in those who do not immediately fit the middle-class stereotype, or are there more complex questions to ask, such as 'What is the relationship between class, gender, ethnicity, educational qualifications, and first language? Are some church traditions or parts of church tradition more open to identifying vocation? Are there prejudices among congregations, selection boards, or even bishops?'

Certainly it would be wrong to argue that linking the Ordained Local Ministry Scheme to higher education accreditation has caused the switch, since many on the course would have been exploring vocations to ordination with their Diocesan Director of Ordinands prior to Southwark's Scheme being validated by the University of Wales (Bangor). The vision of Mervyn Stockwood's worker-priests seems as far away as ever, except that many OLMs are workers, but now in a fast-changing and technological world where some of the old class and social barriers are being dismantled, and the Church is following rather lamely behind and is clinging to outmoded attitudes to class and educational attainment. It is interesting to observe that some former ordinands who were given extra academic support while training are the very people who have become inspired by the learning process and are continuing their studies to degree level.

Resources

When I was appointed as Principal of the Ordained Local Ministry Scheme, some three years ago, my parents, from a very practical farming background, asked me, 'Well, what else do you do?' Somehow managing and sharing in some of the teaching associated with the training of 20 to 30 ordinands, and assisting 20 of those already ordained in a degree programme, looked like a part-time job. The questioning felt even more pointed than for those of us as parish priests who are used to people commenting, 'Yes, I can understand what you do on a Sunday, but what do you do during the rest of the week?' If I had dared to say that, apart from me, there were 70 other people helping in the delivery of this programme, then they might have found it very hard to hold back from saying 'Get a life!' Perhaps to some it looks a bit of a small enterprise: a sledgehammer to crack a nut. The reality is, of course, if the number of ordinands and students were quadrupled, the amount of extra work involved for the core staff would be negligible, since so many basic resources have to be in place regardless of student numbers. For Southwark the resources are immense, and many of them are hidden costs. There is, however, a two-way flow of benefit, because as the Ordained Local Ministry Scheme receives the services of tutors and other staff grounded in local experience, so also tutors are encouraged to keep up to date with their own studies and to further develop specialisms.

Financial costs

Ordained Local Ministry Schemes in England are a financial partnership between the diocese (and perhaps parishes) and the central body of the Church of England. There is a block grant (regardless of the size of the Scheme) of about £7,500 per annum and a grant of £700 per ordinand. (This is a tiny grant compared to that given for those training through residential colleges and regional courses.) The diocese then provides further funds to enable Southwark's Ordained Local Ministry Scheme to have a full-time Principal, a part-time Vice-Principal, and some administrative support. Other professional services are occasionally bought in – for example, voice training. On top of this, the diocese provides premises for classrooms, an office base and a library. In recent years Southwark parishes sponsoring ordinands have also been asked to contribute towards the cost, to the tune of £600 per candidate.

Services in kind

Beyond the most obvious financial support, there are areas of massive hidden costs. We recently conducted a survey of voluntary staff associated with the Southwark Ordained Local Ministry Scheme. The average hours worked by each of these people in a year is given in brackets after their job. There are teaching tutors, some of whom deliver whole modules and others who oversee modules taught by a number of tutors (2.8 hours' time commitment associated with each hour of face-to-face contact with ordinands). There is a placement supervisor (90 hours per annum), university co-ordinator (60 hours per annum) and librarian (60 hours per annum). There are year tutors associated with each cohort (200 hours per annum), peer group facilitators for groups within cohorts (13 hours per annum) and academic support tutors (24 hours per annum) who assist ordinands who have limited formal education or who have a special need, e.g. dyslexia. Each ordinand has a ministry team facilitator associated with their team in the parish (17 hours in year 1) and a pastoral tutor (13 hours per annum).

Clearly, some tutors, such as pastoral tutors, have time costs largely associated with being present at meetings, but for others there may be considerable preparation time, as in the case of someone producing teaching material for the first time; and then there is the annual updating, not to mention marking, second marking, staff development, and individual tutorials with students. Even for the most experienced teachers, for every hour spent in front of a class there is considerable non-contact time spent in preparation and marking. This means that in an average year the number of voluntary hours given to the Scheme is the equivalent of a further two full-time staff members. In addition to this group of voluntary staff there are many other people involved in running the Southwark Ordained Local Ministry Scheme: for instance, staff at the University of Wales (Bangor), people on management committees, and people in ministry teams in the parishes.

The regionalization of training

All of this might change when plans for regionalization of training are implemented. The plans envisage different types of training institution in each region interacting both formally and informally. Distinctions between ways of training may become less straightforward with this greater interconnectedness. The General Synod Report *Formation for Ministry within a Learning Church*[20] proposes dividing England into eight 'Regional Training Partnerships' (two in the province of York and six in the province of Canterbury). Southwark falls in the south-east region and includes the Dioceses of Southwark, Rochester, Canterbury and Chichester. It is far too soon to say what the implications of these new Regional Training Partnerships will be for the training of OLMs, but clearly links will be developed with partners in the region – that is, other training institutions in other dioceses and the regional training course. (There is no residential training college in the south-east region.) Also within the diocese there is likely to be increased co-operation between courses. Currently Southwark Ordained Local Ministry Scheme is validated by a university not just outside the region, but outside the province; there may be pressures to realign validation internally to the region, though in an increasingly internet age it hardly matters if an institution is 50 miles away in Canterbury or 250 miles away in north Wales.

Conclusion

The Southwark Ordained Local Ministry Scheme is continually adapting to new circumstances as the context changes. The future of such schemes in the new regional patterns of training is unknown, particularly since they are often small training units. Ordained Local Ministry Schemes generally, and Southwark's in particular, offer a gift to the whole Church. They use individual, personal experience as one of the foundations of theological reflection in a way that offers enormous potential for individual growth; they connect theology and the world; their integrative and holistic approach covers both process and product; and their stress on collaboration prepares ordinands for the realities of ordained parish ministry.

No training institution, though, can function in isolation. Perhaps it is Ordained Local Ministry Schemes that can help the wider Church to consider issues of selection, recruitment and leadership and to move to approaches that are free of prejudice and injustice, so that we might become a Church that is truly inclusive and representative. Ordinands from Southwark Ordained Local Ministry Scheme relish their commitment to lifelong learning and are inspired by the educative and integrative process of theological reflection and learning. A hundred good priests, deacons and ordinands are tribute to the vision that brought Southwark's Scheme into being. Ordained Local Ministry is, and will be, a significant part of the Church of England in the twenty-first century.

Further reading

Stranger in the Wings: A Report on Local Non-Stipendiary Ministry, Advisory Board of Ministry Policy Paper no. 8, Church House Publishing, London, 1998.

Archbishops' Council, *Mission-shaped Church: Church Planting and Fresh Expressions of Church in a Changing Context*, Church House Publishing, London, 2004.

Formation for Ministry within a Learning Church (GS 1496), Church House Publishing, London, 2003.

Notes

1 *Formation for Ministry within a Learning Church*, GS 1496 (the Hind Report), Archbishops' Council, Church House Publishing, London, 2003.

2 *Stranger in the Wings: A Report on Local Non-stipendiary Ministry*, Advisory Board of Ministry Policy Paper no. 8, Church House Publishing, London, 1998.

3 *Stranger in the Wings*, p. 77.

4 *Rule of Benedict*, chapter 58.

5 Belbin, R. Meredith, *Management Teams: Why They Succeed or Fail*, Butterworth Heinemann, Oxford, 1981.

6 *A Review of LNSM Schemes: Developments of Models of Ministry and Training in Recent Diocesan Proposals for LNSM*, Advisory Board for Ministry (ABM) Ministry Paper no. 4, London, 1992.

7 Kolb, D., *Experiential Learning*, Prentice-Hall, Englewood Cliffs, New Jersey, 1984.

8 Groome, T. H., 'Theology on Our Feet: A Revisionist Pedagogy for Healing the Gap between Academia and Ecclesia', in Mudge, Lewis S. and Poling, James N., *Formation and Reflection: The Promise of Practical Theology*, Fortress Press, Philadelphia, 1987, p. 75; Lartey, E., 'Practical Theology as a Theological Form', in Woodward, J. and Pattison, S. (eds), *The Blackwell Reader in Pastoral and Practical Theology*, Blackwell, Oxford, 2000, pp. 128–34.

9 Walton, R., 'Using the Bible and Christian Tradition in Theological Reflection', *British Journal of Theological Education*, vol. 13, no. 2, 2003, pp. 133–51.

10 Pattison, S., Thompson, J. and Green, J., 'Theological Reflection for the Real World: Time to Think Again', *British Journal of Theological Education*, vol. 13, no. 2, 2003, pp. 119–31, p. 128.

11 The Archbishops' Council, *Formation for Ministry within a Learning Church: The Structure and Funding of Ordination Training – an Update*, Church House Publishing, London, 2004, p. 11. This indicates that a task group has been set up to look at the 'parameters for the curriculum' for 'ordinands in the pre-ordination and post-ordination phases'.

12 Advisory Board of Ministry, *Education for the Church's Ministry: The Report of the Working Party on Assessment*, ACCM Occasional Paper no. 22, Advisory Board for Ministry, London, 1987.

13 Advisory Board of Ministry, *Beginning Public Ministry: Guidelines for Ministerial Formation and Personal Development for the First Four Years after Ordination*, ABM Ministry Paper no. 17, Advisory Board for Ministry, London, 1998, p. 5.

14 Leslie, D., 'Transformative Learning and Ministerial Education in the Church of England – Some Examples of Appropriate Ways of Engaging the Public Realm in the Context of Late Modernity', *British Journal of Theological Education*, vol. 14, no. 2, 2004, pp. 168–86, p. 171.

15 Farley, E., *Theologia: The Fragmentation and Unity of Theological Education*, Fortress Press, Philadelphia, 1983. Farley speaks of theology as 'habitus' or 'wisdom for living'.

16 Chopp, R. S., *Saving Work – Feminist Practices of Theological Education*, Westminster John Knox Press, Kentucky, 1995, p. 17.

17 'Reform' is an Anglican society drawing from the evangelical tradition and upholding what it sees as traditional, biblical

principles; and 'Forward in Faith' draws from the catholic wing of the Church and strongly opposes the ordination of women as priests.

18 Macpherson, Sir William, *Report of an Inquiry* (The Macpherson Report), the Stationery Office, London, 1999, Cm 4262-I. See Summary Chapter 46, §27.

19 Ousely, Sir Herman, *Report of an Independent Inquiry into Institutional Racism within the Structures of the Diocese of Southwark*, Commission for Racial Equality, Diocese of Southwark, London, 2000.

20 Ministry Division of the Archbishops' Council, *Formation for Ministry within a Learning Church: The Final Report on the Regions*, GS Misc 745, Archbishops' Council, London, 2004, Appendix 4.

13. Realizing Potential

JUDITH ROBERTS

The kingdom of heaven is like a mustard seed that someone took and sowed in his field; it is the smallest of all the seeds, but when it has grown it is the greatest of shrubs and becomes a tree, so that the birds of the air come and make nests in its branches. (Matthew 13.31–2)

Inherent in ministerial training is the assumption that everyone has potential for further development. In other words, ordinands have to aspire to and attain something new in their own lives, both in relation to their own spiritual journeys and in their relations with other people, their parishes, their friends, their families, their peer groups in ministerial training, the hierarchy of the Church, and with God. It is our responsibility on the Southwark Ordained Local Ministry Scheme to facilitate this process of self-development, while at the same time putting in place the academic and practical content of the course and contributing to the process of assessment that will determine whether the ordinand is ready or even suited to becoming a priest.

We all think we know and understand the word 'potential' and most educationalists use it freely. But of course a chapter about 'potential' needs a definition, and immediately the difficulties begin. The *Concise Oxford Dictionary* defines the word thus: 'the capacity for use or development' and 'possibility'. In isolation, neither of these definitions is exciting, but once they are conjoined then a glimmer of light emerges. Southwark Ordained Local Ministry Scheme (alongside, I trust, the selection procedures for ordination in the Church of England) does embrace whole-heartedly the concept of growth and development and the many possibilities in this process leading towards the highest achievement and transformation within training.

Hazel Whitehead (Principal of the Guildford Diocese Ministry Course Scheme) says this:

Most GDMC students don't reach their full potential whilst in training but go some way towards it. Certainly, they begin to recognize and work towards it. This happens through the liberation which comes from new understanding, new friendships, new responsibility, new ownership of calling and through very hard work – in study, prayer and personal development. The contribution of the peer group and other groups is vital; they would not do it alone.

She has got to the heart of the matter: potential is part of a lifelong process, and it comes along with dedication, commitment and engagement with others. The key issue of 'process' is central; no two ordinands start or finish at the same point, but all ordinands are involved with a focused training that enables significant growth in knowledge, understanding and skills. This development allows the principals of training courses to recommend to the appropriate bishop that the ordinand is ready to embark upon ordained ministry.

For over 25 years I, and countless other teachers, when writing school reports, have used the word 'potential' euphemistically. The intention was to offer a marginal upgrade on phrases such as 'could do better', 'must try harder' or 'needs to engage more fully with the subject'. The phrase 'has potential' indicates that the pupil is underachieving and needs to do some work. But it also suggested that there could be a magic moment when that potential was reached. In the school context, this could mean that an exam or benchmark had been passed. But often the way the word is used in school reports does not do justice to how 'potential' is being used in this chapter, with the strong sense of process and continuing development.

Any attempt to realize the potential of an ordinand must start with some assessment of what that potential might be. It is, of course, possible to start with a woolly notion of potential and just hope that the Scheme with its various support structures and challenges, both academic and personal, will lead to progress. However, it is far preferable to work through the setting of some goals and targets for achievement. How these targets and goals are set and met is central to the Southwark Ordained Local Ministry Scheme, alongside the support that is given for these to be achieved.

Prior to starting ordination training, students will have engaged with, and survived, the selection process. Rightly so, this procedure is demanding, rigorous and all-embracing, and the selectors' reports give some indication of present attainment and expectations for the future; they also indicate where there might be possible weaknesses that will need extra support. These reports are significant as they are the culmination of a considerable process in which ordinands have already explored vocation and grappled with the many complexities surrounding this. Alongside the reports are individuals' self-perception: their hopes, concerns, aspirations and fears. Southwark OLM ordinands come from diverse backgrounds of ethnicity, language, geography, education, church tradition, etc. What they share in common, regardless of their existing qualifications and experience, is that they have all responded to an inner call, and that they have all been encouraged by their parishes and recommended by the Church of England. They embark upon this journey of discovery together, and the richness of diversity stimulates and challenges them throughout the training.

In the sections that follow I will endeavour to integrate descriptive theory with practical examples. (Issues of confidentiality arise, but I hope to use examples in a way that does not reveal identity, but allows for understanding.)

Southwark's approach

Practice

Southwark's approach is unashamedly one of 'praxis'. It takes very seriously ordinands' existing knowledge, understanding, skills and experience and uses this as the starting point for moving on to further learning. Ordinands grow in confidence when they use their own practice as the benchmark from which to move to further understanding, knowledge and self-development. This approach encourages (and in fact requires) considerable theological reflection and study to integrate practice and theory. By engaging with others, both on the course and in the parish, all ordinands learn to ask questions, make connections, discover alternatives and be open to new insights about themselves and the many tasks they face. This approach, plus involved and inspiring teaching and tutoring, offers ordinands a fruitful way to realize their potential during the training process. The other dimension, not surprisingly, is the commitment and engagement of individual ordinands.

Academic issues

A significant reason for Southwark Ordained Local Ministry Scheme exploring university accreditation was the concern of ordinands that, in a modern Britain where nearly 50 per cent of the population are graduates, their training might seem to be under-valued. Negotiations with the University of Wales (Bangor) allowed the Southwark Course to submit its modules (with their strong emphasis on praxis) for accreditation. The first cohort graduated in 2003 with diplomas in ministerial studies. This included 14 former students who returned to upgrade their quali-fications. One of the strengths of the Bangor Scheme is that Southwark Ordained Local Ministry Scheme writes the material most appropriate for ordinands in training in the diocese.

Not surprisingly, the Church of England expects its ordinands to be well educated (and to achieve recognizable standards within theological education) and to develop a commitment to lifelong learning. Southwark Ordained Local Ministry Scheme offers an integrated training that allows individual ordinands to engage with serious study both individually and in partnership with others. This integration covers what they learn and how they learn it. It is our aim for all our students to reach diploma level, and further degree studies are offered to those who, after ordination, want to continue to study in a way that continues to combine theory and practice. With energy, commitment, stringent reflection and determined study, the ordinands are challenged and sup-ported to further their intellectual development while achieving the necessary academic level.

It is unlikely that a system will ever be found that will be ideal for everybody, but the Southwark system certainly has a multi-faceted approach, allowing for a wide range of existing knowledge, practice and experience to be used. Nevertheless, the individual who is happiest surrounded by books and who finds engagement with people more daunting will be challenged by our approach. They will find that academic attainment will be judged both on the work they submit individually and the work they do in peer groups. Similarly, students who enjoy constant discussion, with very little substance to it, will be strongly encouraged, even directed, to widen their learning strategies. Ordinands are expected to be 'adult learners' and to take individual responsibility for their assignments. No assignment can be completed without collaborating with others, and ordinands quickly become aware of how much they can learn from one another. The concept of 'collaboration' is not going to go away, because it is fundamental to training and to parish ministry later on.

Transformation/personal development

'Yesterday has gone, tomorrow is not here and so there is today.' This was said in a video produced in 1998 by the Spires Centre, a centre for homeless people and those with alcohol and drug dependencies, in Streatham in South London. It captures what transformation is about, how there is movement from the past through the present to the future, and what matters is what you do with the present. Clearly this is true for all of us, as well as for our ordinands. But a key issue for us in assessment relates to how individuals develop over the training period and how this is demonstrated.

Yearly reports attempt to both quantify and qualify this. Here there is a genuine attempt to gauge what development has occurred and how this has been transformative. Some of the information is purely descriptive; for example, the modules they have studied and the marks given. Ordinands are encouraged from the outset to keep a 'learning journal'. This is confidential to them, and is an opportunity to include very personal thoughts and feelings. This can become a rich reservoir for the self-reflection that the ordinands offer in their yearly self-reflective reports.

Further reports come from the parish and from the year tutor, year facilitator, Vice-Principal and Principal. The final report is comprehensive, drawing on all the other written reports and responding to the bishops' requirement to cover theological learning, spiritual and ministerial formation, practical preparation for ordained ministry and personal maturity. For example, one subsection about 'awareness of self and others' would include observational details by tutors regarding relational and pastoral skills, feedback from the parish and peer group, information from individual discussions, evidence of how pastoral awareness and skills are translated into practice, and how individual ordinands have reflected upon their learning and experiences and their ability to communicate this. All the ordinands engage in the Myers Briggs workshops (which enable them to recognize differing personality types) and they are familiar with the insights of Belbin (enabling understanding of group dynamics). They are expected to use this knowledge in their reflections about themselves and their relationships with others.

Assessing transformation is not an exact science, but with clear criteria and a willingness to be honest on the part of those assessing and those being assessed, there can be a reasonable expectation that a fair appraisal will be made. On rare occasions an ordinand may not agree with the final assessment, and he/she can state this.

Where there is divergence between the assessor and the ordinand there is often a wonderful opportunity for further reflection and subsequent learning and development!

The balanced approach

The gathering of evidence to support judgements made about ordinands is both objective and subjective. All written work is marked by two tutors, and over the three years a range of people will have contributed to such assessment. This is true also for presentations and practical work. The yearly reports aim at being comprehensive and cohesive by acknowledging attainment and personal development and looking towards further targets. They also highlight specific weaknesses that need to be addressed as a matter of urgency.

Some examples may help to explain this further. There may be an ordinand with little formal education who has achieved above-average marks for written work – this is to be applauded, but a target might be set for the ordinand to reference work properly, include a bibliography, and set out work in a clearer manner, writing in full, grammatical sentences and with accurate spelling and punctuation. Some specific help might be offered to support this.

Another example might be the ordinand who achieves high marks for individual work, but comparatively low marks for group work. There may be a variety of reasons for this, but one of them might be that this ordinand underperforms in a group context. We can offer support to help address this difficulty.

A final example might be the ordinand who is reaching the pass mark, but really not flourishing and apparently underachieving. The yearly assessment would acknowledge this and, after discussion, some strategies might be agreed to help the ordinand improve performance. This could take the form of special academic support or a review of lifestyle and commitments culminating in agreement about the change needed for improvement.

Words such as 'transformation' and 'personal development' are just as difficult to define as 'potential'. Some ordinands are so driven by the need to achieve that their quest for outstanding marks overrides any sense of priestly formation. It takes courage on the part of assessors, tutors and other ordinands to persevere with confronting the ordinand with this reality. Of course, it is encouraging to observe ordinands grappling with the purely intellectual content of the course, but this has to be balanced with self-awareness and pastoral understanding and skills. Attitudes can and do change, but not without struggle. The 'victim' mentality also has to be challenged. An ordinand might constantly hide behind a belief that because he or she has not been to university, he/she cannot be expected to do the written work without un-realistic amounts of assistance. Patience and resolution is required to challenge and change this mind-set. There are examples of ordinands who began like this but have now matured, having progressed to becoming independent learners, and having chosen to further their education to degree level.

A sense of transformation (again a process) occurs when ordi-nands honestly begin to integrate their knowledge, understanding and skills. This needs very focused self-appraisal and maturity. Some ordinands who start with closed minds resort to tactics such as denial and avoidance, but I have been surprised at how often it is possible to locate trigger points of release that allow them to have the courage to acknowledge their need for change. I would like to be able to claim that the many hours I have spent in deep con-versation with the ordinand have been this trigger point of trans-formation, but my observation is that the peer group has the greater impact. Perhaps my contribution was the groundwork! I am grateful to those course members who, either in humour or more vigorously, have challenged the obsessive, the closed mind, the student who won't listen. Nevertheless, what may at first appear to be a Damascus Road experience is more likely to be the working out of a long and sometimes painful process of self-realization.

Formal structures

Too many structures and the spirit is crushed; too few and the focus is lost. One of the strengths of the Southwark Ordained Local Ministry Scheme is its ability to be flexible and to create structures that effectively meet perceived needs. For the last three years, for example, we have added year tutors to our staff team. These volunteer tutors are all former students or teaching tutors, and their job description commits them to weekly term-time attend-ance, twice-termly staff meetings, the study days, occasional visits to residential weekends, the assessment of weekly worship, and yearly assessment interviews. The strength of this structure is that each year group is well grounded and supported and that pastoral issues can be more readily addressed. They demonstrate collabora-tive working with the Principal and Vice-Principal, and along with the placement supervisor, librarian and university co-ordinator they have become core staff. This is a two-way process; as ordi-nands progress on their own individual journeys, so do staff.

The Scheme has another layer of formal structure that is focused on 'facilitation', both in peer groups and in the ministry teams from the parishes. Again, the Scheme is reliant on volunteers who tend to be former students or people in the diocese who are skilled in this area and who have expressed a wish to be involved. These facilitators are key staff in enabling ordinands to reflect on how groups work in general and how they themselves function in a group. Surprising insights emerge and, through good facilitation, ordinands are challenged to reflect thoughtfully on relational issues and are encouraged to develop accordingly. Facilitators feed into the assessment process.

The yearly assessment is a formal structure which, when used well, can also be a vital part of recognizing and discerning inter-action between progress and potential. Nevertheless, there may need to be more immediate action to attempt to rectify difficulties and problems as they emerge during the year. The recent inspec-tion in 2004 raised this very issue: What interventions do we make to ensure that problems don't just accumulate and become destruc-tive? For example, a year tutor confirmed observation of an ordinand who seemed withdrawn and avoiding contact with others. This was further endorsed by the year group, who came to voice their concerns. Clearly, the issue could not wait for the yearly assessment interview and so a strategy meeting was convened to decide a way forward. So the structures are there for support, but on occasion there is need for flexibility.

Support structures

Alongside the formal structures are the support structures that help ordinands on their journeys of transformation. A key rela-tionship is that of the pastoral tutor. This is a *confidential* relation-ship. Ordinands meet with the pastoral tutor twice termly to discuss their progress and possible concerns. The Principal and Vice-Principal meet once a year with pastoral tutors (who are OLMs, parish priests, Readers, spiritual directors) to discuss the course and new developments generally in theological education, and also to listen to general feedback. Ordinands find their relationship with their pastoral tutor highly supportive as they grapple with new learning and understanding.

Another form of support structure is afforded by the academic support tutor. Sometimes the selection report has already indi-cated that extra academic support will probably be needed. During the introductory term we make a judgement and offer an academic support tutor, who works in a one-to-one relationship and helps to guide the planning and writing of assignments. On other occasions individual ordinands make their own requests for extra support. Since the Scheme began, 15 out of 100 course members have been supported in this way, mainly by former OLM students with a teaching background. Initially, it was one of my roles – and one I relinquished reluctantly because there is considerable satisfaction in working closely with an enthusiastic person who gradually makes progress. (I remember an ordinand who presented me with a thick, red, felt-tipped pen as a thank you for extra lessons and for all the red ink I had offered her!) Ordinands who have had little formal education often need extra help with written English. Those whose first language is not English are similarly helped, as well as those who may be dyslexic or lacking in confidence. Occasionally, we offer individuals intensive academic support. Nevertheless, ordinands are not expected to arrive at their academic support tutors with a blank page and a blank brain!

Most training courses are for three years, but Southwark has an introductory term and this has proved to be valuable. The original suggestion came from former students who explained that it was a long wait from the selection conference to the beginning of the academic year and that they would rather engage with study straight away. The opening module, 'Theology in Context', helps to earth the ordinands and allow them to get to know each other, the structures, the relationship between Scheme and home parish, the patterns of working and some tools for theological study. This introductory term can also 'iron out' misconceptions and 'iron in' expectations!

The role of the Vice-Principal

Although it was my choice and desire to focus on the issue of potential, I nevertheless approach this section with trepidation. My job description is a river in spate; the problem with good ideas and insights is that they require considerable work, effort and energy – a realizing of potential perhaps! It became apparent that I had a key oversight and responsibility in relation to the concept of potential. Of course, I am not working in isolation regarding this issue, but I try to keep 'potential' on the front burner and to make connections with all the other structures and people involved with the ordinands. The role of a Vice-Principal is a curious one, and one that can sometimes feel like running just to keep up. Perhaps I like running, and perhaps I'm fortunate to have excellent people around me who have a sense of ministry that allows them to engage with the teaching and learning process, thus allowing for their own continuing development and nurturing that of others.

The only reason that I can thrive in this role is because the Principal is a keen exponent of collaborative working, recognizes there is too much to do, and has a sense of humour! This has allowed me to develop structures and practices that are not just filling gaps, but finding effective ways forward to enabling the ordinands to flourish and to grow in self-awareness as they accumulate knowledge and build on previous skills. I work in a climate that encourages creativity, connectedness and exploration and this is just as true of staff as it is of ordinands. I also have a role in maintaining a proper rigour in marking and personal assessment, a task that is often uncomfortable but necessary.

Transferable skills

Much of my adult life was spent in primary school teaching in the inner city, culminating in headship 1977–90. Theological students often present many of the same concerns as young people in educational settings! Organizing school life and managing the immediate day-to-day issues has certainly contributed towards my daily input on the Scheme. Marking, assessment, extra support, discipline, pastoral care, review, planning, challenging, encouraging, etc., are firmly in the bloodstream. For me, the interactive style of teaching in primary schools has proved to be very valuable in opening up theological concepts and debate with theological students.

We live in a rapidly developing technological era that demands effort and training to keep afloat. Furthermore, our world is changing and there are pressing issues such as globalization, ecological awareness, inter-faith dialogue and inclusion clamouring for recognition and a place in the already very crowded syllabus. Alongside this, there are demands for serious study of gender, race, culture, disability and sexuality. So my own education and reading has continued in recognition that previous knowledge, skills and understanding are always in need of refinement and development. So, as I continue with my journey of realizing potential, I interact with students, tutors, incumbents, facilitators, etc., who are on a similar quest.

My time as a headteacher coincided with the requirement for a plethora of policy documents covering all aspects of school life. This has not abated (our inspection document was over 5,000 words). One significant memory remains with me from those days: I had incorporated the discipline policy paper within the pastoral care policy. This apparently quite disconcerted officialdom, and an interesting dialogue ensued. But I continue to maintain that 'pastoral care' embraces all aspects of development, including the need for strong critique, benchmarks and firm comment, including sanctions. The Southwark Ordained Local Ministry Training scheme has high expectations of its ordinands, both in terms of personal development and of academic achievement. It is also prepared to spend time, energy and resources to support those who at some time in their training may need this. This ranges from formal structures to the more informal 'check out' approach initiated usually by the Vice-Principal in discussion with the year tutor and Principal.

'Check out' initially appears to be an innocuous statement, but it can cover some quite confrontational issues. Occasionally, for example, an ordinand is fixated on achieving exceptional (and maybe unrealistic) high marks, and there is the inevitable crisis when the mark given is disappointing. An appeal to adult maturity is not always immediately effective, so time is spent bringing the ordinand to a better understanding and resolution. A quite robust and even confrontational approach over a series of meetings might well be required. In contrast to this is the ordinand who is under-achieving but who has not had the courage to initiate discussion regarding issues at home, work, parish, or health issues, which bear on this. Again, one may spend a similar amount of time, but with a different approach. The aim in both instances is for the ordinand to reach self-awareness and understanding coupled with a desire and strategy for change.

One of the many joys of being Vice-Principal of the Southwark Ordained Local Ministry Scheme is that of observing the development of nearly 100 individual ordinands. Our responsibility is to provide a coherent training that will equip the ordinands for ministry by building on existing knowledge, understanding and skills and requiring significant engagement with biblical material, the traditions of the Church, the power of reason, and personal experience. As ordinands grapple with new material, different teaching methods, doubts, and challenging personal relationships, we discern real and profound development and a sense of excitement and enjoyment of the training process. This can only support the transformation process. It is not always a smooth passage!

A few examples will indicate the hazards on route. Most ordinands knuckle down and wholeheartedly engage because they recognize that it is in their best interests to do so, but there have been the occasional individuals who are convinced they know better. This is demonstrated in a range of ways, including not involving themselves with peer group working because they feel it is beneath them – not an ideal attitude for collaborative working. Another example is when the belief that women should not be in positions of authority either in society or in the Church interferes with full participation. This has led to some interesting debate and a real opportunity for the integration of biblical study and Church traditions with modern understanding. Uniformity of opinion is certainly not wanted, but ordinands do need to learn to present reasoned positions and to give evidence rather than ill-thought-out prejudice. Occasionally ordinands arrive on the Scheme with closed minds and then work incredibly hard to preserve that position. It becomes our task to challenge this and to work with the ordinands: not to refute them, but to seek balance and perspective.

Conclusion

Attitudes, ability, values and gifts are what we have to work with, and it is how these interact and connect that enables ordinands to grow in faith and knowledge so that they will be ready to move on to the next part of their ministry in ordained capacities. I have witnessed amazing transformations. I really believe that theological training courses in general, and Southwark's Ordained Local Ministry Training Scheme in particular, contribute not only to individual development but to the continuing renewal of the Church. Individual ordinands are given the opportunity and responsibility of witnessing to a gospel of justice, freedom and reconciliation in their homes, churches, places of work and communities – genuinely realizing their potential.

Further reading

Ackroyd, R., and Major, D., *Shaping the Tools – Study Skills in Theology*, Darton, Longman and Todd, London, 1999.

Adair, J. and Nelson, J., *Creative Church Leadership*, Canterbury Press, Norwich, 2004.

Belbin, R. Meredith, *Management Teams: Why They Succeed or Fail*, Butterworth Heinemann, Oxford, 1981.

Cassidy, S., *Audacity to Believe*, Collins, London, 1977.

Craig, Y., *Learning for Life: A Handbook of Adult Religious Education*, Mowbray, London, 1994.

Exley, K. and Dennick, R., *Small Group Teaching Tutorials, Seminars and Beyond*, Routledge Falmer, London, 2004.

Freeman, R. and Lewis, R., *Planning and Implementing Assessment*, Routledge Falmer, London, 1998.

Griffin, J., and Tyrrell, I., *Human Givens – A New Approach to Emotional Health and Clear Thinking*, HG Publishing, London, 2004.

King, P., *Leadership Explosion: Maximising Leadership Potential in the Church*, Hodder and Stoughton, London, 1987.

Kroeger, O., and Thuesen, J.M., *Type Talk*, Delacorte Press, New York, 1988.

Peck, M. Scott, *The Road Less Traveled: A New Psychology of Love, Traditional Values and Spiritual Growth*, Simon & Schuster, New York, 1978.

Peck, M. Scott, *In Search of Stones: A Pilgrimage of Faith, Reason and Discovery*, Hyperion, New York, 1997.

Conclusion: Redrawing the Landscape

MALCOLM TORRY AND JEFFREY HESKINS

... if this plan or this undertaking is of human origin, it will fail; but if it is of God ... (Acts 5.38–9)

In the spring of 2005 the authors of this book met to reflect on the chapters they had each contributed. Two things in particular emerged from the day.

At the end of our time together someone noticed that, quite independently of each other, several contributors had used the phrase 'here to stay', and it became clear that this was how some of us had come to experience Ordained Local Ministry. In adopting the notion of an Ordained Local Ministry, the Church has redrawn part of the landscape of the historic priesthood. A criticism that some people make of Ordained Local Ministry is that it seems to defy a fundamental principle of the priesthood in a catholic tradition – namely, that priests are trained and ordained to go anywhere, live anywhere, and minister anywhere. Ordained Local Ministry challenges that hitherto unchallenged view. Our thoughts on the experience of the first ten years of the Scheme do not so much contradict this view of the priesthood as invite all of us to adjust our view of what the ordained ministry might be. What Ordained Local Ministry does is give an additional dimension to the concept of ordained ministry rather than detract from it or weaken it. Ordained Local Ministry, as we have experienced it and reflected upon it, retains a strong sense of commitment, but one in partnership with a local community. That community knows that the priest called out from among them, trained in the midst of them, and returning to minister in a very particular way to them, is one who is here to stay.

We also sensed that, as a concept, this invaluable innovation in our understanding of priesthood and local ministry is neither a fleeting whim to address a declining trend in vocations to ordination by making the route simpler, nor an attempt to provide clergy on the cheap. It is instead a concept that will allow the

Church to step into the future. As a concept it too is here to stay.

The second thing to emerge from our day together was a very buoyant sense of hope for a Church facing change. Explicitly this book charts changes in the landscape of the Church's ordained ministry, but implicitly it is about people and their communities. Many of the people we encounter in this book might seem quite unremarkable and may seem to come from unremarkable places, and the same might be said of the authors of the book's chapters: but as we consulted with one another, some of us knew that we were spending time with some remarkably gifted people who have given, and are giving, their lives to a remarkable and historic period of change in the life of the Church of England. It is that boldness to make change in the face of change that marks this particular initiative out as special.

The world is changing, and Ordained Local Ministry has emerged at a time of considerable change for the Church. In 1994, women were ordained priest for the first time in the Church of England (and quite a lot of those priests are OLMs, partly because lower age barriers prevented older women from considering other routes). Although we cannot claim to live in a classless society, the coherent working class that the Stepney Scheme was all about no longer exists. We now experience socio-economic diversity, cultural diversity and ethnic diversity, resulting in a complex matrix of backgrounds. This is the society from which Ordained Local Ministry candidates are drawn, and they reflect that diversity. Many inner-city Anglican congregations are now mainly black, and Ordained Local Ministry reflects this.

The last 20 years have seen Ordained Local Ministry become an important and valued component of the life of the Church in many dioceses. Mature candidates, with plenty of life experience to offer, have been selected and trained and they are faithfully serving their parishes. Bishops who have initially not been persuaded of the benefits of Ordained Local Ministry have often been persuaded by the quality of ministry offered by OLMs. There are now similar schemes in New Zealand, Australia, Canada and the USA; and the practice-based educational model is now a growing feature of courses in a variety of residential and part-time ministerial training courses.

And there is more change on the way. Training for ministry in the Church of England is becoming regionalized, with different training institutions in each area being expected to co-operate with one another. Maybe by the time this book is published major changes will have been decided upon and implemented. What is clear is that, on the evidence of this book, Ordained Local Ministry training schemes will make a significant contribution to future training for ordained ministry, and we hope that what we have written will inform future discussion of Ordained Local Ministry training and practice.

When something ceases to be an experiment there is always a danger of atrophy. We don't believe that this will happen. A ministry rooted in the Church's parishes – in their communities and their congregations – is in a good position to adapt to changes in our society and in the Church; and an educational model rooted in practice is in a good position to train people for relevant ministry.

Our book has been mainly about the Diocese of Southwark's Ordained Local Ministry. We hope that our readers will make links with their own context and their own experience so that together we shall be able to give God thanks for the ministry of OLMs and their parishes, and for those who support, select and train them – and so that together we shall be able to extend this ministry and see it evolve so that it might continue to serve our communities and their congregations.

Appendix 1: Appointments in parishes where there is a pattern of shared ministry, a ministry for mission team, or an Ordained Local Ministry[1]

Notes for those involved in making appointments

The appointment of a new incumbent in a parish where there is a commitment to shared ministry and team working is crucial to the effective working of the parish. Local Non-Stipendiary Ministers (LNSMs) are ordained on the understanding that their ministry will be exercised within a parish in the context of a shared or collaborative style of ministry. Experience suggests that the time following the appointment of an incumbent is the most critical point in the life of a team or the ministry of a LNSM (OLM).

But what is shared ministry? Shared ministry is about every Christian being called to share in God's ministry in the world. This leads to shared leadership within a congregation where the aim is to free the gifts of all the baptized for service in Christ.

In order to illustrate what we mean, here is an example of styles based on a hypothetical ministry to those who are housebound or sick in a parish. All these styles may be evident in a person's ministry but for effective working with a team, the ability to minister in the collaborative or enabling model is absolutely essential:

- 'Individual' – incumbent visits a sick parishioner.
- 'Advisory' – incumbent gathers people together who reflect on the needs of the sick.
- 'Delegated' – incumbent asks a parishioner to go and visit a sick person and report back to him/her.
- 'Collaborative or shared' – team and incumbent decide who is the appropriate person to visit and share reflections on the visits.
- 'Enabling' – parish visitation ministry is administered by the team or parishioners.

There is a need for a person who can take the initiative but is not overly competitive or arrogant. When asking questions about past ministry, look for the word 'we' rather than 'I'. One of the main misunderstandings which people have is in the area of 'shared' and 'delegated' authority.

Many clergy look upon a host of people doing a multitude of jobs and reporting back as shared ministry. The incumbent with this style of 'delegated' authority can have an enormous amount of control over a congregation. This can be a major source of frustration and anger in a team where decisions, policy and reflection on issues have taken place in a team setting. An enabling ministry is creative, but just to make sure that the candidate is an enthusiastic worker and not a shirker, look for someone who:

1 Can share faith – the ability to be open about one's faith is essential for good team working.
2 Can show how they have worked creatively with others in past ministry or employment.
3 Is secure in his/her sense of self. A sign of spiritual maturity is when people are secure enough to help others develop their gifts beyond their limitation. An incumbent in a context of shared ministry needs to be capable of dealing with conflict, loss and criticism, while being aware of his/her own vulnerability and weakness.

Note

1 Reprinted from *Stranger in the Wings: A Report on Local Non-Stipendiary Ministry*, Advisory Board of Ministry Policy Paper no. 8, Church House Publishing, London, 1998, pp. 41–2.

Appendix 2: Ordained Local Ministry Scheme Statistics

Table A.1   The proportion of ordinands training on Ordained Local Ministry Schemes

Year	Residential colleges	Regional courses	OLM Schemes	OLM Schemes as percentage of total	Total
1990	761	442			1203
1991	761	446			1207
1992	750	455			1205
1993	677	455			1132
1994	623	473	58	5%	1154
1995	542	510	87	8%	1139
1996	512	561	135	11%	1208
1997	533	574	170	13%	1277
1998	601	594	193	14%	1388
1999	638	615	201	14%	1454
2000	622	596	204	14%	1422
2001	614	598	191	14%	1403
2002	552	609	217	16%	1378
2003	505	596	217	16%	1318
2004	501	638	169	13%	1308

Source: Ministry Division (Sarah Evans)

Note: There has been a rise in the number of OLMs over the short period they have existed. This appears to have plateaued out. Is 2004 a blip or the beginning of a decline?

**Table A.2   Year 2002–03: Ordinands in different types of
training institutions in the Church of England**

Number of institutions	Type of institution	Total number of ordinands	Average per institution	Percentage male
19	OLM Schemes	217	11	42%
12	Regional Courses	586	49	38%
11	Theological Colleges *	549	50	68%
42	All Institutions	1352	32	51%

* These figures do not include Llandaff or TISEC (Theological Institute for the Scottish Episcopal Church).

Source: *Formation for Ministry within a Learning Church*, GS 1496 (the Hind Report), Archbishops' Council, London, 2003, pp.149–50.

Notes: There are 19 dioceses with OLM Schemes in England recognized by the House of Bishops in the Church of England. This represents just under half the dioceses of the Church of England.

Southwark OLM Scheme is unusual in that it only trains ordinands. Most other Schemes train ordinands alongside other ministries such as Readers.

The size of OLM Schemes, taking them simply as a statistic relating to ordinands, is small.

It is significant that colleges (and therefore training of stipendiary clergy) are still dominated by men.

Table A.3 Sponsored OLM candidates training on Schemes recognized by the House of Bishops 2002–03

Diocese	Men	Women	Total	2000–01
Blackburn	2	4	6	5
Canterbury	7	10	17	15
Carlisle	1	3	4	3
Coventry	2	2	4	2
Gloucester	3	2	5	5
Guildford	6	9	15	12
Hereford	4	2	6	3
Lichfield	8	4	12	13
Lincoln	1	4	5	1
Liverpool	1	5	6	6
Manchester	7	11	18	18
Newcastle	1	1	2	2
Norwich	8	13	21	21
Oxford	9	9	18	16
St Eds and Ips	7	7	14	7
Salisbury	6	16	22	28
Southwark	12	18	30	27
Truro	0	0	0	2
Wakefield	5	7	12	5
Total	**90**	**127**	**217**	**191**

Source: Formation for Ministry within a Learning Church, GS 1496 (the Hind Report), Archbishops' Council, London, 2003, p. 150.

Note: Southwark OLM Scheme has 27 ordinands, which makes it larger than two theological colleges at this period (Queen's, Birmingham: 21; and St Stephens House, Oxford: 22) and two courses (Carlisle and Blackburn: 12; and East Midlands: 25) and the largest OLM Scheme in terms of ordinands.

Table A.4 Southwark OLM attendance at selection conference for OLM ministry, 1992–2005

Type of selection conference	Selected	Not selected	Overturned on Appeal
Local	108	17	5
National	8	3	2 *
	116 (85%)	20 (15%)	7 (5%)
Total (%)	136 ** (100%)		

* One was overturned by the Bishop of Chelmsford
** A number of potential ordinands went to more than one conference. Those eventually being accepted are *not* recorded as 'not selected'. In fact, 142 selection places have been used by potential OLMs from Southwark.

Source: Diocesan Data, Ministry and Training Department

Notes: Southwark has a level of success in sending ordinands to selection conferences.

In September 2005, Southwark's OLM Scheme had its first ordinand from another diocese (Chelmsford).

Table A.5   Southwark OLMs in Training: cohort size, age, marital status, gender and race *

Cohort	Number in cohort	Average age per cohort	Married ratio (Number widows/ divorced)	Number male (%)	Number Ethnic minority students
1992–5	7	58	6	6 (86%)	1
1993–6	7	51	3	3 (38%)	0
1994–7	5	55	2	4 (80%)	1
1995–8	9	50	6	5 (67%)	0
1996–9	8	49	3 (1)	6 (75%)	0
1997–2000	7	54	5	2 (29%)	1
1998–2001	10	53	9	6 (60%)	0
1999–2002	7	57	6	6 (86%)	1
2000–03	13	57	10	5 (38%)	4
2001–04	11	50	8	5 (45%)	2
2002–05	7	55	6	2 (29%)	1
2003–06	7	55	5 (2)	3 (43%)	2
2004–07	8	54	6 (1)	1 (13%)	2
2005–08	12	47	10	6 (50%)	2
Overall	118	53	85 (72%)	60 (51%)	17 (14%)

* All those completing the first year of training are included, whether ordained or not.

Source: Diocesan Data, Ministry and Training Department

Notes: The typical profile of an OLM: the average age is 53 years; they are just as likely to be female as male; and they are likely to be married with an average of 2.7 children.

Table A.6 Southwark OLMs entering training: employment category

Employment category	Number	Percentage
Manager and senior officials	24	20%
Professional	37	31%
Associate profession and technical	10	9%
Administrative and secretarial	9	8%
Skilled trades	2	2%
Sales and customer services	7	6%
Elementary	1	1%
Self-employed	4	3%
Homemaker	4	3%
Retired	20	17%
All categories	118	100%

Source: Diocesan Data, Ministry and Training Department

Notes: The type of job a candidate has is not always clear from the way they complete the form. This table give an indication of OLMs' socio-economic background.

The overwhelming impression given of those entering OLM training is of professional and often managerial staff, secure in their employment, or those recently retired.

Table A.7 Distribution of OLMs in Diocese of Southwark (October 2004)

Episcopal area	Archdeaconry	Deanery	Y1	Y2	Y3	Ord	Total
Croydon	Croydon	Addington	1			2	3
		Central	1			4	5
		North	1	1		1	3
		South				4	4
		Sutton		2		4	6
		Sub-total	**3**	**3**		**15**	**21**
	Reigate	Caterham				1	1
		Godstone				4	4
		Reigate			1	9	10
		Sub-total			**1**	**14**	**15**
Kingston	Lambeth	Brixton				1	1
		Clapham		1		1	2
		Lambeth			1	1.5	2.5
		Merton				4	4
		Streatham	1			2	3
		Sub-total	**1**	**1**	**1**	**9.5**	**12.5**
	Wandsworth	Battersea	1			1	2
		Kingston			1	4	5
		Richmond and Barnes				2	2
		Tooting		1		5	6
		Wandsworth				1	1
		Sub-total	**1**	**1**	**1**	**13**	**16**
Woolwich	Lewisham	Charlton			3	2	5
		Deptford				4	4
		E. Lewisham	1	1	1	2	5
		Eltham and Mottingham				3	3
		Plumstead	1			2	3
		W. Lewisham				3	3
		Sub-total	**2**	**1**	**4**	**16**	**23**
	Southwark	Bermondsey				3	3
		Camberwell				3	3
		Dulwich				1	1
		Southwark and Newington	1	1		2.5	4.5
		Sub-total	**1**	**1**		**9.5**	**11.5**
Southwark		**Total**	**8**	**7**	**7**	**77**	**99**

Source: Diocesan Data, Ministry and Training Department

Note: There is no deanery in the diocese where there is not an OLM present.

Table A.8   Details of OLM candidates in training as at October 2004

	Y1	Y2	Y3	Total
Under 40	0	0	0	0
41–50	2	1	1	4
51–60	5	4	4	13
Over 60	1	2	2	5
Male	1	3	2	6
Female	7	4	5	16
White	6	5	6	17
Minority ethnic	2	2	1	5
Further education/professional qualifications	8	5	7	20
No further study after school	0	2	0	2
Full-time employment	3	5	5	14
Part-time employment	3	1	1	4
Unemployed	0	0	1	1
Retired	2	1	0	3
UPA*	3	5	2	10
Non-UPA	5	2	5	12

From 2004: parishes in IMD** Red zone. From 2004, the government reclassified areas of deprivation. The UPA category is no longer in use and it has been replaced by zones of Indices of Multiple Deprivation. The diocese currently has less than half of its parishes in IMDs as compared with the number of UPA parishes (64 IMD: 133 UPA).

* UPA: Urban Priority Area
** IMDs: Areas with high Indices of Multiple Deprivation replacing UPAs (Urban Priority Areas)

Source: Diocesan Data, Ministry and Training Department

Table A.9   Details of Southwark OLMs as at October 2004

Age at ordination		
Under 40	5	
41–50	12	
51–60	32	
Over 60	28	
Male	42	(55%)
Female	35	(45%)
White	68	(88%)
Ethnic minority	9	(12%)
Pre-2004: parishes UPA/non-UPA: *		
UPA	27	(35%)
Non-UPA	38	(49%)
From 2004: parishes in top IMDs/not in top IMDs **		
Red zone	2	(3%)
Not in Red zone	10	(13%)

* UPA: Urban Priority Area
** IMDs: Areas with high Indices of Multiple Deprivation replacing UPAs (Urban Priority Areas)

Source: Diocesan Data, Ministry and Training Department

Note: The Diocese of Southwark has become more prosperous over recent years and the number of parishes falling into areas recognized as having high Indices of Multiple Deprivation has dropped. There are, however, pockets of deprivation that are masked by the figures that deal with rather large units.

Other facts

Ethnicity
Of the 20 people from ethnic minorities over the years 1992–2005 (9 African background, 9 West Indian background, 2 other), none have been born in this country.

Readers
34 of OLMs were Readers prior to entering the OLM Scheme. This was particularly evident in the early years of the OLM Scheme.

Glossary

Accreditation A process by which Ministry Division approves theological colleges, courses and schemes for training ordinands, either following the writing of a plan for a new institution or following inspection of an existing institution (re-accreditation); or a process by which a university agrees that students following another institution's course can be granted degrees of the university.

Advisory Council for the Church's Ministry (ACCM) A council that advised the bishops on training for ministry and ran selection conferences to enable it to recommend candidates to the bishops for ordination. It was replaced by the Advisory Board for Ministry (ABM), which has now been replaced by Ministry Division.

Alpha course A course of study for enquirers published by Holy Trinity, Brompton. The course consists of a series of evenings during which participants share a meal, listen to a talk, and hold a discussion. There might also be a weekend about the Holy Spirit.

Altar A table at which, according to Jesus' command, bread and wine are taken, thanks is given, bread is broken, and the bread and wine are shared. It is called an 'altar' because the stone construction on which animals were slaughtered during and before the time of Jesus was called an 'altar'.

Anglican The Anglican Communion is all those dioceses that are in communion with the Archbishop of Canterbury: in practice, all those whose bishops attend the Lambeth Conference once every ten years.

Anglicanism A set of practices and ideas that characterize the Anglican Communion, or more specifically, the Church of England.

Archbishops' Council A council chaired by the Archbishops of Canterbury and York which was set up to streamline the government of the Church of England.

Archdeacon A bishop's assistant, with legal and other functions of their own but which can be delegated. An archdeacon must be in deacon's orders, but is usually a priest. In practice, an archdeacon can be a pastoral figure in the diocese.

Area See 'Episcopal Area', except when used in 'area dean' when it means a deanery.

Area Dean A new name for a Rural Dean.

Baptism The initiation rite for a Christian. It can be carried out at any age, but when a child is baptized, godparents speak for them.

Benefice A parish or parishes of which a priest is incumbent.

Bishop Someone ordained by other bishops to the first order of the Church's threefold ministry of bishop, priest and deacon. The bishop acts as a focus of unity for the diocese and cares for its people and clergy. A diocese always has a diocesan bishop, and might also have suffragan (meaning assistant), area, or assistant bishops.

Bishops' Advisory Panel A three-day residential event at which candidates for ordination are interviewed by Bishops' Selection Advisers and during which they undertake a number of individual and group exercises. The panel makes recommendations to candidates' bishops as to whether or not candidates should train for ordination.

Bishop's Council A diocesan body that formulates policy ready for decision by the Diocesan Synod, and that has the authority to take decisions over such matters as how many churchwardens a particular team ministry can have.

Bishops' Selection Adviser Someone appointed by the House of Bishops to interview candidates during Bishops' Advisory Panels and to participate in making decisions as to whether or not candidates should be recommended for training.

Black-led church	A congregation or federation of congregations with a predominantly black leadership. The membership is normally predominantly black as well. The ethos tends to be Pentecostal.
Board	A body appointed by a synod or synods to oversee particular areas of the Church's life in a diocese or nationally.
Candidate	Someone who believes that they might have a vocation to ordination and is testing that vocation through the Church's selection procedures and initial training.
Catholic	Used as a term to describe the worldwide Church. In the historic creeds, it means 'universal'. It is most frequently used to describe that part of the Church led by the Bishop of Rome (the Roman Catholic Church), but it is also used by some others who adhere to more ornate and ritualistic forms of worship.
Chalice	A large cup, usually of silver or silver plated, into which wine is poured at the Eucharist and from which the congregation drinks.
Chaplain	Someone fulfilling a pastoral role in an institution, usually a hospital, factory, university, etc. The chaplain might or might not be a member of the clergy.
Chapter	A regular meeting of the clergy of a deanery that they are expected, but not obliged, to attend.
Children's church	What a church's children and children's church teachers do while the Sunday morning service is happening. Different age groups often meet in different rooms, and activities might include prayer, singing, listening to biblical and other stories, cutting things out, gluing things, and colouring in pictures.
Church	With a lower case initial letter, it means a congregation of Christians or the building within which they meet. With a capital initial letter, it means the entire universal body of Christian believers and all of its local manifestations. The word can also have a capital letter if it is part of a denomination's title, as in 'Methodist Church'. In many

contexts in this book, the word will start with a capital letter because it is short for 'Church of England'. The word also has a sociological meaning: see below on 'Denomination'.

Church Army A voluntary hierarchical organization that evangelizes, runs homelessness projects, and generally lives out the gospel. Best understood as the Anglican version of the Salvation Army. Hence 'Church Army evangelist': 'evangelist' because they are commissioned as evangelists; and 'Church Army officer', which means 'Church Army evangelist'.

Church of England A federation of dioceses in England that have bishops in communion with the Archbishop of Canterbury and, since dioceses are federations of parishes with umbrella organizations to serve them, the Church of England is a federation of parishes and of umbrella organizations.

Church Times An independent newspaper carrying news and opinion about the Church of England and worldwide Anglican Communion matters.

Churchwarden An ancient elected office. Each parish has two churchwardens elected annually. The churchwardens have a number of powers, such as the ability to veto the appointment of an incumbent, and a number of responsibilities, such as the annual completion of articles of enquiry sent by the archdeacon. They are responsible, with the incumbent, for the maintenance of public worship and the care of the church building.

Clergy A collective noun for bishops, priests and deacons. Whether the clergy remain laypeople is an interesting question. A priest remains a deacon, and a bishop remains a priest and a deacon, so it might be thought that they all remain laypeople. But the Church's synodical structure separates people into bishops, other clergy, and laity.

Common Worship The name of the collection of alternative services authorized for use in the Church of England in 2000.

Communion
Sharing in bread and wine at the Eucharist, from which derives the meaning of 'taking communion to . . .': usually to someone who can't get out and to whom a priest or someone else takes bread and wine from the service in church. See also: 'Anglican'.

Confirmation
The bishop lays his hands on the candidate's head and prays for the Holy Spirit to 'confirm' them. Historically this action was part of a single baptismal rite. Confirmation is either administered to people who were baptized as infants and now wish to 'confirm' the promises previously made on their behalf, or it immediately follows baptism as an adult. Normally only people who are confirmed (or are ready to be confirmed) receive communion. But now members of other denominations are also welcome to receive communion.

Congregation
Any gathering of Christians for the purpose of worship.

Continuing Ministerial Education (CME)
Training that clergy are expected to undertake after they've been ordained.

Course
A training course; though when used in 'theological course', it can either mean any theological training course or an institution training people part-time for stipendiary or non-stipendiary ministry.

Curacy
An assistant priest's post. An assistant priest in a parish can be either stipendiary or non-stipendiary. The term often applies to an ordained minister's first and training post where the curate is under the supervision of a training incumbent. For the first year, the curate is a deacon and thereafter a priest.

Curate
Someone undertaking a curacy.

Daughter church
A building and congregation established in another part of the parish by the 'mother church'.

Deacon Someone ordained by the bishop to the third order of the Church's threefold ministry of bishop, priest and deacon. The deacon's role is outlined in the Ordinal and is one of service and teaching. The deacon cannot preside at the Eucharist, hear confessions, absolve someone from their sins, or be incumbent of a parish. In the Church of England someone has to be a deacon for a year before they are ordained priest, though some people are selected to be permanent deacons.

Deanery An area, sometimes coterminous with a natural community or communities but not always, usually comprising a dozen or so parishes. Every deanery has a Deanery Synod (chaired by the lay chair and the area dean) and a clergy chapter (chaired by the area dean).

Deanery Synod The governing body of a deanery.

Denomination A federation of congregations, usually with an umbrella organization or organizations to fulfil functions best carried out centrally, such as the payment of clergy. The word also has a separate but connected meaning in the social sciences, where it means a category of religious organization between the categories of 'sect' and 'church'. The denomination has more open boundaries than a sect, but boundaries less open than for a church (with 'church' here defined in terms of characteristics such as open boundaries and diverse belief-systems, i.e. not as defined above).

Deployable Ministers are 'deployable' when a bishop can decide where they are to be licensed once they're ordained. Because Ordained Local Ministers (OLMs) return to the parishes within which they were selected for training, they are not deployable.

Diocesan missioner Either a canon of the cathedral or someone else whose job it is to remind the parishes that mission is their responsibility. They might do some mission themselves.

Diocesan Synod	The governing body of a diocese. There are three houses: bishops, clergy, and laity. A vote by houses can be requested. The synod sets diocesan policy and the budget of the diocese. All bishops in the diocese are members, and there are elections for the house of clergy (among all clergy) and for the house of laity (the electors being Deanery Synod members).
Diocese	A federation of parishes with an umbrella organization to carry out those functions best dealt with centrally. The chief pastor of a diocese is its bishop (who might be assisted by suffragan or area bishops)
Diocese of Southwark	The parishes of South London and of parts of Kent and Surrey.
Director of Ordinands	Someone who encourages people to explore vocations to the ordained ministry, pilots them through the selection process, keeps in touch with them through their training scheme, and allocates them to curacies.
District	In a parish with more than one church building, districts can be established. The Parochial Church Council (PCC) can delegate to District Church Councils certain decisions relating to particular buildings, the congregation that meets in it, and the Church's mission in the community in which the building is situated.
District Church Council	The governing body of a district. The Parochial Church Council (PCC) of the parish in which the district lies decides which decisions to delegate to the District Church Council.
Doctrine	Teaching: so in this context the content of what the Church has agreed to believe and teach.
Ecumenism	The relating of different denominations to each other at local, regional or national level.
Elder	The churches that Paul and others founded during the first Christian century were governed by elders: older respected members of the congregation. Some denominations retain this name for those who govern a congregation.

Electoral roll A list of all those who live in the parish, or who worship regularly in the parish church, who declare their wish to be on the roll by completing an application form. Only those on the roll are eligible to vote at a parish's Annual Parochial Church Meeting, which elects the Parochial Church Council (PCC). It's the nearest thing the Church of England has got to a membership list. In order to fill in the form you have to declare yourself to be a member of the Church of England or of a Church in communion with it.

Episcopal area Part of a diocese in which some of the diocesan bishop's functions have been delegated to an area bishop.

Eucharist A fourfold action of taking bread and wine, giving thanks over them, breaking the bread, and sharing the bread and wine. The word's meaning generally extends to the whole event, including hymns, readings, prayers, the peace, etc.

Evangelical A Christian or a congregation might be called evangelical if they think of the Bible as the Christian's primary authority. Evangelical worship is often informal.

Evangelism The proclaiming of the good news of the kingdom of God's coming.

Evangelist Someone who specializes in telling the good news of the kingdom of God's coming.

Evening Prayer An evening service containing Bible readings, canticles (biblical passages said by the congregation), and prayers.

Evensong Evening Prayer with some parts sung, and maybe hymns added.

Examining chaplain Someone appointed by the bishop to examine candidates for ordination. Their role is to interview candidates after a Director of Ordinands has seen the candidate several times. The Director of Ordinands might ask the examining chaplain to explore particular issues with the candidate.

Facilitator Someone who helps a group or an institution to function better, usually by feeding back observations on the dynamics of the group or institution.

Faith community	Any body of people who are adherents of a religion.
Father	A male parent; the name Jesus used for God; a designation for a male priest.
Free Church	This term normally designates any denomination apart from the Church of England and the Roman Catholic Church, e.g. the Methodist Church. There are many non-affiliated congregations that can be regarded as Free Churches in their own right.
Freehold	A priest who is inducted as rector or vicar (or team rector) holds the freehold of the benefice. This is a useful legal fiction. It means that the incumbent owns the parish church and the parsonage house, but can't do anything with them except look after them. (A priest who holds the freehold can stay in post until they are 70 years old.)
General Synod	The national governing body of the Church of England. There are three houses: bishops, clergy (but not bishops), and laity. A measure has to pass in all three houses if a vote by houses is requested. The synod sets national policy and the budget of the Church's central departments. All diocesan bishops are members, and there are elections for the House of Clergy (among all clergy) and for the house of laity (the electors being Deanery Synod members).
Gospel	Good news of Jesus and of the kingdom of God for which he hoped and which he proclaimed.
Healing ministry	Praying for people who are ill or otherwise suffering, the prayer often being accompanied by the laying on of hands and/or anointing with oil. These actions might take place in someone's home, in a hospital, or at a service in church.
Higher education	Education of a more academic nature for people over 18 years of age.
Hind Report	*Formation for Ministry within a Learning Church*, Church House Publishing, London, 2003. John Hind, Bishop of Chichester, chaired the commission that wrote the report.

Holy Communion	See 'Eucharist'.
Holy Spirit	The third person of the Trinity. For this and other theological terms, readers should consult a good theological dictionary.
House group	A gathering of Christians in someone's home for the purpose of Bible study, prayer and discussion, usually on a regular evening each week or fortnight.
House of Bishops	The term can either mean all the bishops who sit in a particular synod, or just the diocesan bishops.
House of Clergy	The members of clergy elected to a synod, apart from the bishops, who have a house of their own.
House of Laity	The members of the laity elected to a synod. Clergy cannot be members of the house of laity even if they might still be members of the laity.
Incumbent	The priest who holds the freehold of the benefice.
Industrial chaplain	A chaplain in an industrial institution, though in practice many industrial chaplains undertake a variety of activities in connection with the Christian faith's relationship to the economy.
Industrial mission	The activity of relating the Christian faith to the world of work and to the economy. An industrial mission is an institution set up for this purpose.
Initial training	Training that candidates are obliged to undertake before they can be ordained. The usual pattern is two or three years in an accredited institution.
Inner London Education Authority (ILEA)	ILEA was in charge of schools in London's inner boroughs until the government dispersed this responsibility to the Borough Councils.
Inspection	An inspection of a theological college, course or scheme, by a team of inspectors appointed by Ministry Division on behalf of the House of Bishops.
Intercessions	Prayers, normally offered during public worship, requesting God to do things, though the word sometimes refers to private prayer.

Inter-faith	A description of worship or other activity in which institutions and/or members of different faiths are involved. Because inter-faith activity such as joint worship might distress members of individual faith communities, such activity tends to be small-scale, and for individuals committed to inter-faith work. Sometimes civic events (e.g. after riots or bombings) are held, but these events tend not to be called worship.
Interparochial clergy	Clergy, whether licensed to particular parishes or not, whose work takes them, with the bishop's permission, across parish boundaries.
Kingdom of God	The just and peaceful reign of God, and the heart of Jesus' gospel and of Christians' evangelism.
Laity	Anyone other than bishops, priests and deacons. Whether bishops, priests and deacons remain laity after their ordination is an interesting question.
Lambeth Conference	A conference convened once every ten years to which the Archbishop of Canterbury invites every bishop whom he believes to be in communion with him.
Lay chair	Parochial Church Councils (PCCs) and synods have clerical chairs and lay chairs. In the case of the PCC, the lay chair only chairs when the clerical chair isn't present. In synods, lay and clerical chairs usually alternate.
Lay reader	An old name for a Reader.
Layperson	A member of the laity.
Licence	A document giving a deacon, priest or reader permission to fulfil their ministry in a particular parish or parishes.
Liturgy	What is said and/or done at church services, though the word sometimes refers to an agreed and printed wording for services.
Local Ecumenical Partnership	A formally constituted relationship between churches (buildings and/or congregations) of different denominations. Provision is often made for joint worship within certain limits.

Local Non-Stipendiary Minister (LNSM)	A previous designation of an Ordained Local Minister (OLM).
Local Ordained Minister (LOM)	A previous designation of an Ordained Local Minister (OLM).
London Docklands Development Corporation (LDDC)	A body set up by government to take control of the development of previous dockland areas of London. In areas given to the LDDC to control, normal local authority planning permission processes ceased to apply.
Mass	See 'Eucharist'.
Measure	Legislation passed by General Synod and approved by Parliament.
Methodist Church	A denomination started by some of John Wesley's followers.
Minister	A rather loose term to refer to anyone undertaking a liturgical or pastoral function. The minister can be a bishop, a priest, a deacon, a Reader, a Southwark Pastoral Auxiliary, or another layperson. The word means 'servant'.
Minister in secular employment (MSE)	A non-stipendiary priest who sees the focus of their ministry in their place of work rather than in the parish to which they are licensed.
Ministry Division	See 'Advisory Council for the Church's Ministry'.
Missa Normativa	The Roman Catholic liturgy for the Mass.
Mission	Going out to serve and evangelize. Hence 'mission team': a group of people in a parish or diocese trained and commissioned to do mission.
Missioner	Someone who does mission, or helps others to do so.
Morning Prayer	A morning service containing Bible readings, canticles (biblical passages said by the congregation), and prayers.
Mother church	See 'Daughter church'.

Multi-faith	A description of activity in which institutions and/or members of different faiths are involved. Unlike 'inter-faith', joint activities that might distress members of the faith communities involved are avoided.
Muslim	An adherent of Islam, the religion founded on the Qur'an and of which Muhammad is the final prophet.
Neighbour-hood profile	A description, in words, pictures, tables and graphs, of the neighbourhood in which someone will function as an Ordained Local Minister (OLM).
Non-Stipendiary Minister (NSM)	A deacon or priest who does not receive a stipend. Most non-stipendiary clergy are curates and are usually designated 'honorary curate'.
Office	Morning Prayer and Evening Prayer are offices.
Office for Standards in Education (OFSTED)	A government body responsible for inspecting schools.
To ordain	To make someone a deacon, priest or bishop. See 'Ordination' below.
Ordained Local Minister (OLM)	A minister ordained deacon and then priest following a diocesan training course. The licence usually restricts the minister's role to a particular parish or parishes.
Ordained Local Ministry Scheme	Either a scheme establishing Ordained Local Ministry in a diocese, or short for 'Ordained Local Ministry Training Scheme'.
Ordained Local Ministry Training Scheme	A training course to prepare people for Ordained Local Ministry.
Ordinand	Someone who has been selected for training for the ordained ministry.
Ordination	The act of making someone a deacon, priest or bishop. This is done by the bishop (or, in the case of the ordination of a bishop, bishops) laying hands on the candidate and praying that God's Spirit will give him/her the necessary grace for the office and work of the ministry in question.

Parish	The parish is a patch of land with its community and institutions, with a congregation or congregations, with a priest or priests, and with a building or buildings for worship.
Parish communion	See 'Eucharist'.
Parochial Church Council (PCC)	The governing body of a parish. The church-wardens and the incumbent are *ex officio* members. Members are elected from the electoral roll at the Annual Parochial Church Meeting. The Council takes all decisions relating to the life of the parish except for a few reserved to the incumbent (mainly in relation to the conduct of worship).
Pastoral	Anything to do with the care of a parish's or an institution's people in the context of a religious tradition, or with a parish's organization or boundaries, or with the structures within which clergy operate. Hence 'pastoral auxiliary': someone appointed to do pastoral work.
Pastoral care	The care of a parish's or an institution's people, that care employing the resources of a religious tradition.
Pastoral studies	The study of things pastoral.
Pentecost	A Jewish festival. At the Pentecost immediately following Jesus' resurrection, the Holy Spirit descended on the apostles and the Christian Church was born.
Pentecostal	A description of congregations or federations in which the spiritual gifts mentioned by Paul in 1 Corinthians 12 and 14 (and particularly speaking in tongues) are central to prayer and worship.
Permission to officiate (PTO)	A bishop's authorization of a priest to preside and preach in his diocese. Retired clergy (aged 70 plus) are usually granted permission to officiate, and some others are too.
Petertide	St Peter's Day, 29 June, and the seven days following: a traditional period for ordinations.

Placement	The placement of a student or trainee in an institution, for a defined number of hours during a defined number of weeks, for an educational purpose.
Post-Ordination Training (POT)	A previous designation for the first three years of Continuing Ministerial Education (CME).
Praxis	Another word for 'practice'.
Presbyter	Greek word for 'elder'.
Priest	Someone ordained by the bishop to the second order of the Church's threefold ministry of bishop, priest and deacon. The priest's functions are outlined in the Ordinal.
Priest in charge	A priest appointed to a parish either with a fixed-term licence or with no security at all – so less in charge than a priest with the freehold.
Privy Council	One of the oldest institutions of government in the UK. Appointment is for life, but only ministers of the government of the day participate in its policy work. Schemes for pastoral reorganization in the Church of England, for the redundancy of church buildings, and for various other matters, have to be agreed by the Privy Council.
Province	A federation of dioceses. One of the province's bishops is designated its archbishop. In England there are two provinces, Canterbury and York.
Quiet day	A day during which there are periods of silence, often interspersed with talks or services.
Reader	Someone trained in preaching and in leading worship (but not the Eucharist) and licensed by the bishop to fulfil these functions in a parish or parishes.
Rector	One of the two designations of an incumbent of a parish. The other is 'vicar'. Historically, the vicar stood in for a rector.
Regional course	Courses, such as the South-East Institute for Theological Education, serving a region rather than a single diocese.
Retreat	A period for reflection, often away from home.

Roman Catholic Church A federation of parishes and dioceses in communion with the Bishop of Rome.

Rural dean A priest appointed by the bishop to convene the clergy chapter and chair the Deanery Synod. There is some debate as to whether the rural dean is the bishop's representative to the deanery or the deanery's representative to the bishop. In practice, he or she is usually a bit of both.

Sacrament An outward and visible sign of an inward spiritual reality. The Church of England recognizes two sacraments instituted by Christ: baptism and the Eucharist. The Roman Catholic and other Churches recognize another five.

Sacristan Someone who prepares the altar, linen, vessels, bread and wine, etc. for the Eucharist and cares for linen and vessels.

Scheme In this context: either short for a scheme for Ordained Local Ministry in a diocese; or short for a course training people for Ordained Local Ministry.

Second Vatican Council A Council of the Bishops of the Roman Catholic Church called by Pope John XXIII. Many of its documents, issued between 1962 and 1965, brought the Church into closer contact with the modern world and with other denominations. The question of follow-through is another matter.

Selection Conference A previous designation for a Bishops' Advisory Panel.

Selector A previous designation for a Bishops' Selection Adviser.

Seminary See the definition at the beginning of Chapter 9.

Series 3 Alternative forms of liturgy for the Eucharist, initiation services and other services, following previous revisions (series 1 and 2). Series 3 was superseded by the Alternative Service Book in 1980.

The South East Institute for Theological Education (SEITE) A part-time training course for the ordained ministry serving the Dioceses of Southwark, Canterbury, Rochester and Chichester, and also the Methodist and United Reformed Churches. It replaced the Southwark Ordination Course.

Sidesperson   Someone elected at the Annual Parochial Church Meeting to assist the churchwardens in welcoming people to services, taking the collection, guiding people as they receive communion, and counting the money.

Southwark Ordination Course (SOC)   A part-time training course for the ordained ministry established in 1962 for the Diocese of Southwark. It was replaced by SEITE.

Southwark Pastoral Auxiliary (SPA)   Someone trained in pastoral work and authorized by the bishop to serve in a parish or parishes in the Diocese of Southwark.

Spirituality   That aspect of our lives that we might call spiritual.

Stipend   What parochial clergy are paid. It is not a salary as there is no contract of employment. The payment is intended to enable the priest and his/her family to live without financial anxiety and thus to be of service to the parish.

Synod   A gathering of elected and *ex officio* members for deliberation and decision-making. The Church of England has synods at the parish level (Parochial Church Council (PCC)), the deanery level (Deanery Synod), the diocesan level (Diocesan Synod), and the national level (General Synod).

Synodical   Anything to do with synods.

Tabernacle   A cupboard, either behind the altar or freestanding, in which some of the elements of bread and wine consecrated during the Eucharist are reserved so that they can be used for home communions.

Team ministry   A team of clergy, comprising a team rector and team vicar(s), serving a parish or parishes. The team rector is the incumbent, and the team vicar(s) are not. They are all told that they are of incumbent status.

Team rector   Every team ministry has a team rector who is expected to fulfil a co-ordinating role. The team rector holds the freehold of the benefice for a limited period, usually for seven years. The team rector is not a rector.

Team vicar	Every team ministry has one or more team vicars. A team vicar is of 'incumbent status', as is the team rector. The team vicar is not a vicar, but can be designated vicar of a particular parish or district.
Theological college	A residential college for training people for the ordained ministry.
Theological course	A course of study about theology, though it often means a part-time training course for stipendiary and non-stipendiary deployable ordained ministry.
Theology	Words about God.
Title	That part of a curacy that has to be completed before a stipendiary priest can be appointed to a post with responsibility. It usually lasts two years. Non-stipendiary clergy and Ordained Local Ministers (OLMs) normally have to complete a four-year period, and after this period non-stipendiary clergy can move to another parish. Ordained Local Ministers stay where they are.
Training Scheme	A course on which people train for the Ordained Local Ministry.
Tutor	Course staff member. On Southwark Diocese's Ordained Local Ministry Training Scheme there are teaching tutors, year tutors (one for each year group), academic support tutors (to help people struggling with academic work) and pastoral tutors (one for each candidate).
United Reformed Church	A Free Church formed in 1972 from a merger of the Congregational Church and the Presbyterian Church in England.
Validation	A process whereby a university agrees to grant degrees following students' successful completion of another institution's course of study.
Vicar	One of the two designations of an incumbent of a parish. The other is 'rector'. Historically, the vicar stood in for a rector. (A team vicar or a team rector can also be designated vicar of a parish or a district even though neither is a vicar or a rector.)

Vocation   A sense of being called by God to a particular task. Often the word on its own refers to a vocation to be a priest, but it shouldn't.

Word and sacrament   The two main aspects of a priest's liturgical role: preaching God's word and presiding at the sacraments of baptism and Eucharist.

Word, service of the   A service of readings, prayers, hymns and sermon, but no Eucharist.

Worker priest   Now known as Minister in Secular Employment.

Wychcroft   The Southwark Diocesan Training Centre and retreat house set in the midst of farming land in Surrey.

Youth worker   Someone who runs activities for young people or simply gets to know them and listens to them. It might be a full- or part-time activity, paid or voluntary, and under the auspices of a Local Education Authority, a church, or a charity.